# 1600+

# Essential Japanese Phrases

## Easy to Intermediate

## Pocket Size Phrase Book for Travel

By

Fluency Pro

**Disclaimer**

Without the publisher's prior written consent, no portion of this publication may be reproduced, stored in a retrieval system, or transmitted in any form or by any means, electronic, mechanical, photocopying, recording, scanning, or otherwise, except as permitted under Sections 107 or 108 of the United States Copyright Act of 1976. Although every precaution has been taken in preparing this book, the publisher is not liable for any mistakes, omissions, or damages resulting from the use of the material included within. This book is intended solely for entertainment and educational purposes. The opinions presented are those of the author alone and should not be construed as professional advice or directives. The reader's activities are his or her own responsibility. The author and publisher take no responsibility or liability for the purchaser or reader of these contents. The reader is responsible for his or her own usage of any products or techniques referenced in this publication.

*1600+ Essential Japanese Phrases*
First Edition: March 26, 2023
Copyright © 2023 Caliber Brands Inc.
Cover images licensed through Shutterstock.

# Table of Contents

# INTRODUCTION

Welcome! This book can serve as a compact and portable resource for learning Japanese anywhere. This book will help you improve your comprehension of grammar and sentence structure by expanding your vocabulary and enhancing your pronunciation while traveling by air, rail, or bus.

The majority of the population of Japan speaks Japanese because it is the official and national language there. Communities of Japanese people can be found all over the world, from the USA and Canada to Brazil, Peru, Argentina, Australia, New Zealand, the Philippines, Taiwan, and even the UK, France, and Germany. Nevertheless, there are Japanese-speaking groups in nations like South Korea, China, and the Philippines due to immigration.

The subject, then the object, then the verb: this is the standard order for Japanese sentences, known as the subject-object-verb (SOV) pattern. As an illustration, the Japanese phrase for "I eat sushi" is "私は寿司を食べます" (Watashi wa sushi o tabemasu).

Particles are crucial in Japanese for establishing the context of a phrase. Example: the subject of the sentence is indicated by the particle "は" (wa), while the direct object is denoted by the particle を (o).

Several sentence structures can be used in Japanese based on the situation and the intended meaning. To make it clear what the statement is about, the topic might be placed at the beginning of the sentence and then followed by a comma. The verb can also be moved to the conclusion of the phrase if that's where the emphasis lies.

Although the SOV sentence form is consistent, Japanese grammar provides considerable leeway in how sentences are built.

Japanese is spoken in syllables of equal length and stress, with each syllable generated by a different combination of consonants and vowels. The letters "a," I "u," and "e," plus the corresponding sounds, "o" and "u," make up the five vowel sounds in Japanese. Several Japanese consonant sounds are identical to their English counterparts, and vice versa. They include the letters k, g, s, z, t, d, n, h, b, p, m, and y. Nonetheless, the language also features a number of unique consonant sounds, such as the "r" sound, which is made by pressing the tip of the tongue against the alveolar ridge, like the "r" in Spanish. It also features a number of consonant sounds that are easily distinguishable from their English equivalents, such as the letters "sh," "ch," "j," and "ts," which are all pronounced with the same spelling but a more emphatic stress.

**PITCH PATTERNS**

The Japanese language relies heavily on pitch accent patterns for proper pronunciation. The meaning of a sentence can be drastically altered by the way a speaker's voice rises or falls within individual words. Effective communication in Japanese relies heavily on the use of pitch accent, which distinguishes between words that would otherwise sound the same but mean different things.

Each syllable in a word is given a different emphasis based on its position in the word through the Japanese pitch accent system.

Japanese relies on both pitch accent and intonation to communicate meaning. The inflection of a speaker's voice, or intonation, can convey nuanced meanings such as emphasis, emotion, and more. A query may be indicated by a rising intonation at the end of a sentence, whereas a statement may be indicated by a falling intonation. In the midst of a sentence, a rising intonation can signify a list or a continuation of an idea, whereas a falling intonation may signify the finish of a thought.

Another way that the Japanese convey politeness and formality is through the use of pitch. A higher pitch is typically used to indicate politeness and respect in formal settings, while a lower pitch may be utilized in more casual settings. Emotions can also be communicated through pitch, with higher tones representing joy or excitement and lower tones representing grief or rage.

**HOW THIS BOOK IS ORGANIZED**

In this book, you will find over 1600 common Japanese phrases organized by usage or situation.

Each entry follows a standard pattern that gives you the English phrase, the Japanese translation, and a phonetic description of how to pronounce it in Japanese. With the phonetic transcription, you may hear how the Japanese words in print compare to the sounds you already know. Each transcript has been broken down into syllables using dashes. Spaces separate the words. Capitalized syllables receive more emphasis than the lowercase ones.

## ORDERING FOOD

Hi, table for two, please.
こんにちは、2人用のテーブルをお願いします。
Kon-ni-Chi-wa, fu-Ta-ri-yo-u no te-Bu-ru o o-ne-Ga-i shi-Ma-su.

Could we have a booth/table, please?
ブース/テーブルをお願いできますか？
Bu-su/te-bu-Ru o o-ne-Ga-i de-ki-maSu ka?

Can we see the menu list, please?
メニューを見せていただけますか？
Me-nyu-u o Mi-se-te i-ta-Da-ke-mas-K?

Can we see the wine list, please?
ワインリストを見せていただけますか？
Wa-i-n ri-Su-to o mi-Se-te i-ta-da-ke-Mas-ka?

What do you recommend?
おすすめは何ですか？
O-su-su-me Wa na-ni DeSu Ka?

Could we have some water, please?
水をお願いできますか？
Mi-zu o o-ne-Ga-i de-ki-maSu ka?

I'd like to order the salmon, please.
サーモンを注文したいです。
Sa-mo-n o chu-Mo-n shi-Ta-i desu.

Can I have the steak well-done, please?
ステーキをよく焼いていただけますか？
Su-te-ki o Yo-ku Ya-i-te i-ta-da-ke-Mas-ka?

Could I get a side of fries with that?
それにポテトフライをつけていただけますか？
So-re-ni Po-te-to Fu-ra-i o tsu-ke-te i-Ta-da-ke-Mas-ka?

Could we have some more bread, please?
パンをもう少しいただけますか？
Pan o mo-u Su-ko-shi i-ta-Da-ke-Mas-ka?

I'm allergic to nuts, is there any dish without them?
ナッツアレルギーがあります。ナッツを使っていない料理はあ
りますか？
Na-tsu a-re-ru-Gii ga a-ri-Ma-su. Na-tsu

Can we pay separately, please?
別々に支払えますか？
Be-tsu-Be-tsu ni Shi-ha-ra-e-ma-su ka?

This was delicious!
おいしかったです！
O-i-shi-Ka-TTa Desu!

Do you have any vegetarian options?
ベジタリアン向けのメニューはありますか？
Be-ji-ta-ri-an Mu-ke no Me-nyu-u Wa a-ri-Mas-ka?

How spicy is this dish?
この料理はどのくらい辛いですか？
Ko-no ryoo-ri wa Do-no Ku-ra-i ka-ra-i Desu ka?

Can I have a glass of red/white wine?
赤/白ワインを1杯ください。
A-ka/shi-ro Wa-i-n o i-PPai ku-da-sai.

Could we have some more napkins, please?
ナプキンをもう少しいただけますか？
Na-pu-ki-n o Mo-u su-Ko-shi i-ta-Da-ke-mas-ka?

This is not what I ordered.
私が注文したものと違います。
Wa-ta-shi ga Chu-mo-n Shi-ta mo-no to Cha-i-Ma-su.

Can you please heat this up?
これを温めていただけますか？
Ko-re o a-Ta-ta-me-te i-ta-Da-ke-Mas-ka?

Can we have the leftovers to go, please?
残り物をお持ち帰りできますか？
No-ri-Mo-no o o-Mo-chi-kae-ri De-ki-mas-ka?

Excuse me, is the service charge included?
サービス料金は含まれていますか？
Sa-bi-su Ryoo-kin wa fu-Ku-ma-re-Te i-Ma-su ka?

Can we split the bill?
割り勘にできますか？
Wa-ri-Kan ni De-ki-Mas-ka?

Can I get a to-go box for this?
持ち帰り用の容器をもらえますか？
Mo-Chi-Kae-ri-Yo-u

Is service included?
サービス料は込みですか？
Saabisu-ryou Wa komi Desu ka?

Can we have separate checks, please?
別々の勘定にしてもらえますか？
Betsubetsu no Kanjou ni Shite Moraemasu ka?

Can we see the dessert menu, please?
デザートのメニューを見せていただけますか？
Dezāto no Menyuu o Misete Itadakemasu ka?

This dish is too salty.
この料理は塩辛すぎます。
Kono Ryouri wa Shiokara Sugimasu.

Do you have any vegetarian options?
ベジタリアン向けのメニューはありますか？
Bejitarian-Muke no Menyuu wa arimasu Ka?

Thank you, the meal was great.
ありがとうございます、食事はとても美味しかったです。
Arigatou gozaimasu, Shokuji wa totemo Oishikatta Desu.

I would like to orderSelected.
～を注文したいのですが。 ～
o Chuumon Shitai no Desu ga.

Could you please recommend something?
何かおすすめはありますか？
Nanika osusume Wa arimasu Ka?

Can I have a glass/bottle of...?
～のグラス/ボトルをいただけますか？ ～
no gurasu/botoru o itadakemasu ka?

Can we have the bill, please?
お会計をお願いできますか？
Okaikei O onegai Dkimasu Ka?

Can we pay separately/together?
別々に/一緒に支払ってもいいですか？
Betsubetsu ni/ Issho ni Shiharatte Mo ii Desu ka?

Do you accept credit cards?
クレジットカードは使えますか？
Kurejitto Kaado wa Tsukaemasu ka?

How much is it?
いくらですか？
Ikura desu ka?

Could we have some more water, please?
もう少し水をいただけますか？
Mou sukoshi mizu o itadakemasu ka?

# BUYING TRAVEL TICKETS

*Insert the destination, where applicable*

Hi, I'd like to buy a ticket to [destination], please.
こんにちは、[destination] 行きのチケットを買いたいのですが。
Konnichiwa, [ ]-Yuki no Chiketto wo Kaitai Nodesu.

How much is a one-way ticket to [destination]?
片道のチケットはいくらですか。
Katamichi No Chiketto Wa Ikura desu ka.

Do you have any discounts for students/seniors/military?
学生/シニア/軍人向けの割引はありますか。
Gakusei/shinia/gunjin Mukae no Waribiki wa Arimasu Ka.

Can I buy a round-trip ticket to [destination]?
往復のチケットを買えますか。
Oufuku no Chiketto Wo Kaemasu Ka.

Are there any direct flights to [destination]?
[destination]への直行便はありますか。
[ ]-e no Chokkoubin wa Arimasu Ka.

Can I reserve a seat on this flight/train?
この飛行機/列車の座席を予約できますか。
Kono hikouki/ressha no Zaseki wo Yoyaku Dekimasu Ka.

What's the next available flight/train to [destination]?
次に出発する [destination] 行きの飛行機/列車は何時ですか。
Tsugi ni Shuppatsu suru [ ]-Yuki no Hikouki/ressha Wa nanji Desu Ka.

Is there a layover on this flight?
この飛行機には経由地がありますか。
Kono hikouki ni Wa Keiyuchi ga Arimasu Ka.

Can I choose my seat on this flight?
この飛行機の座席は選べますか。
Kono hikouki no Zaseki wa Erabemasu Ka.

What's the earliest flight/train to [destination]?
[destination] 行きの最も早い飛行機/列車は何時ですか。
[ ]-yuki no Mottomo Hayai hikouki/ressha Wa nanji Desu Ka.

Can I change my flight/train schedule?
飛行機/列車のスケジュールを変更できますか。
Hikouki/ressha no Sukejuuru wo Henkou Dekimasu Ka.

What's the latest flight/train to [destination]?
[destination] 行きの最も遅い飛行機/列車は何時ですか。
[ ]-yuki no Mottomo osoi Hikouki/ressha Wa nanji Desu Ka.

How long is the flight/train to [destination]?
[destination] 行きの飛行機/列車はどのくらいかかりますか。
[ ]-yuki no Hikouki/ressha Wa dono kurai Kakarimasu Ka.

Is there a refund policy if I can't make my flight/train?
飛行機/列車に乗れない場合、払い戻しのポリシーはありますか。
Hikouki/ressha ni Norenai baai, Haraimodoshi no Porishii wa Arimasu
Ka.

Do I need to show ID to purchase a ticket?
チケットを購入するためにIDを提示する必要がありますか。
Chiketto wo kounyuusuru tame ni ID wo teiji suru hitsuyou ga arimasu
ka.

Can I get a receipt for my ticket?
チケットのレシートをもらえますか。
Chiketto no Reshiito wo Moraemasu ka.

Is there an extra fee for baggage?
手荷物に追加料金はありますか。
 Tenimotsu ni Tsuika Ryoukin wa Arimasu ka.

Can I check in online?
オンラインでチェックインできますか。
Onrain de Chekkuin Dekimasu Ka.

Can I choose my seat when checking in?
チェックイン時に座席を選ぶことはできますか。
Chekkuin ji ni Zaseki wo erabu Koto wa Dekimasu ka.

How early should I arrive for my flight/train?
飛行機/列車に乗るために何時に到着すれば良いですか。
Hikouki/ressha ni Noru tame ni Nanji ni touchaku sureba ii Desu Ka.

Can I bring a pet on the flight/train?
飛行機/列車にペットを連れて行けますか。
Hikouki/ressha ni Petto wo Tsurete Ikemasu Ka.

Is there a special section for families with children?
子供連れの家族向けの特別な席はありますか。
Kodomo tsure no Kazoku Mukae no Tokubetsu na seki Wa Arimasu Ka.

Is there a vegetarian option for meals on the flight/train?
飛行機/列車の食事にはベジタリアン向けのオプションがあります
か。
Hikouki/ressha no shokuji ni wa bejitarian mukae no opushon ga
arimasu ka.

Can I request a special meal?
特別な食事をリクエストすることはできますか。
Tokubetsu na Shokuji wo Rikuesuto Suru

Is there Wi-Fi on the flight/train?
飛行機/電車にWi-Fiはありますか？
hikouki/densha ni Wi-Fi wa arimasu ka?

Can I buy a ticket to [destination]?
[destination]へのチケットを買えますか？
[ ] e No Chiketto wo Kaemasu Ka?

How much is a ticket to [destination]?
[destination] までのチケットはいくらですか？
[ ] made no Chiketto wa Ikura Desu ka?

When is the next bus to [destination]?
次の [destination] 行きのバスはいつですか？
Tsugi no [ ] yuki no Basu wa Itsu Desu ka?

Where is the bus stop/platform for the bus to [destination]?
[destination] 行きのバスの停留所/プラットフォームはどこですか？
Mokutekichi yuki no Basu no teiryuusho/plattofomu wa Doko Desu ka?

How much does a ticket to [destination] cost?
[destination] までのチケットはいくらですか？
[ ] Made no Chiketto wa Ikura desu ka?

What time is the next train to [destination]?
次の[destination]行きの電車は何時ですか？
Tsugi no [ ] Yuki no densha Wa nanji Desu ka?

How much does it cost to go to [destination]?
[destination]に行くのにいくらかかりますか？
[ ] ni Iku no ni Ikura Kakarimasu ka?

How long will it take to get to [destination]?
[destination]に行くのにどのくらい時間がかかりますか？
[ ] ni Iku no ni Dono kurai Jikan ga Kakarimasu ka?

Can you give me a receipt, please?
領収書をください。
ryoushuusho wo Kudasai.

# EMERGENCY SITUATIONS

I need help.
助けが必要です。
Tasuke ga hitsuyou desu.

I need immediate assistance.
即座の支援が必要です。
Sokuza no shien ga hitsuyou desu.

Someone call an ambulance!
救急車を呼んでください！
Kyuu kyuu Sha wo Yonde kudasai!

This is an emergency!
緊急事態です！
kinkyuu Jitai Desu!

Please help me!
助けてください！
Tasukete kudasai!

I'm in trouble!
困っています！
komatte Imasu!

I'm in danger!
危険です！
Kiken Desu!

I'm hurt!
傷ついています。
kizutsuite Imasu.

I'm injured!
怪我をしています。
kega wo Shite Imasu.

I'm bleeding!
出血しています。
shukketsu Shite Imasu.

I can't breathe!
呼吸できません！
kokyuu dekimasen!

Please call for help!
助けを呼んでください！
Tasuke Wo yonde Kudasai!

Somebody please help me!
誰か助けてください！
Dareka Tasukete Kudasai!

I'm having a heart attack!
心臓発作を起こしています！
Shinzou hossa wo Okoshite Imasu!

I'm having a stroke!
脳卒中を起こしています！
Nousocchuu wo Okoshite imasu!

I'm having an allergic reaction!
アレルギー反応を起こしています！
Arerugii hannou wo Okoshite Imasu!

I'm having a seizure!
発作を起こしています！
hossa wo Okoshite Imasu!

I'm choking!
窒息しています！
Chissoku shite Imasu!

17

Call the police!
警察を呼んでください！
keh-ee-saht-Soo woh yohn-Deh Koo-Dah-sah-ee!

Call an ambulance!
救急車を呼んでください！
Kyoo-koo-Shah woh yohn-Deh koo-dah-Sah-ee!

Call the fire department!
消防局を呼んでください！
Shoh-boo-Kyoh-koo Woh yohn-deh koo-Dah-sah-ee!

Where is the nearest hospital/police station/fire station?
最寄りの病院/警察署/消防署はどこですか？
Moh-yoh-ree noh byoh-een/keh-ee-Saht-soo shoh/shoh-Boo-shoh
wah Doh-koh Deh-soo Kah?

# TECH SUPPORT

My internet connection is slow.
インターネットの接続が遅い。
In-taa-ne-Tto no Se-tsu-Zoku Ga o-so-i.

I forgot my password.
パスワードを忘れました。
Pa-su-Waa-do wo wa-sa-re-Ma-shi-Ta.

The website is not loading.
ウェブサイトが読み込めません。
u-e-Bu-sa-i-to Ga yo-mi-Ko-me-Ma-se-n.

My email account is not working.
メールアカウントが機能していません。
Mee-ru a-ka-un-To ga no-ri-Ko-mi-shi-te i-Ma-se-n.

The printer is not printing.
プリンターが印刷されません。
Pu-ri-n-taa ga in-sa-Tsu sa-re-Ma-se-n.

My computer crashed.
私のコンピュータがクラッシュしました。
Wa-ta-shi no kon-Pyu-ta ga ku-ra-Shu shi-Ma-shi-ta.

The software is not working.
ソフトウエアが動作していません。
So-fu-to-u-e-a ga Do-o-sa-Ku shi-Te i-Ma-se-n.

I am receiving error messages.
エラーメッセージを受け取っています。
e-raa Mes-se-e-ji Wo u-ke-to-te i-ma-su.

The computer is frozen.
コンピュータがフリーズしました。
kon-Pyu-ta ga fu-ri-Zu shi-ma-Shi-ta.

My keyboard is not working.
キーボードが動かない。
Kībōdo ga Ugokanai

I cannot access my files.
ファイルにアクセスできません。
Fairu ni Akusesu Dekimasen

The computer is making strange noises.
コンピューターから奇妙な音がしています。
Konpyūtā kara Kimyōna oto ga Shite imasu

I need to update my software.
ソフトウエアを更新する必要があります。
Sofutowea wo Kōshin suru Hitsuyō ga Arimasu

My computer is infected with a virus.
コンピューターにウイルスが感染しています。
Konpyūtā ni Uirusu ga Kansenshite Imasu

The mouse is not working.
マウスが動かない
Mausu ga ugokanai

I accidentally deleted important files.
大切なファイルを間違って削除してしまいました。
Taisetsuna fairu wo Machigatte sakujo shite Shimaimashita

I need help setting up my new device.
新しいデバイスの設定を手伝ってほしいです。
Atarashii debaisu no Settei wo tetsudatte Hoshii desu

The screen is black.
画面が真っ黒です。
Gamen ga Makkuro Desu

I accidentally spilled water on my laptop.
ノートパソコンに水をこぼしてしまいました。
Nōtopasokon ni Mizu wo Koboshite Shimaimashita

The battery is not charging.
バッテリーが充電されません。
Batterī ga Jūden Saremasen

My computer is overheating.
コンピューターが過熱しています。
Konpyūtā ga Kanetsu Shite imasu

The sound is not working.
音が出ません
Oto ga demasen

I accidentally uninstalled an important program.
大切なプログラムを誤ってアンインストールしてしまいました。
Taisetsuna Puroguramu wo Ayamatte an'insutoru shite Shimaimashita

The internet is not connecting.
インターネットに接続できません。
In-taa-ne-to ni Se-tsu-Zoku de-ki-M-sen.

I need to recover deleted files.
削除されたファイルを回復する必要があります。
sa-ku-jo Sa-re-ta fa-i-ru wo kai-Fuku su-ru hi-tsu-Yo ga a-ri-Ma-su.

My printer is not printing.
プリンターが印刷されません。
pu-ri-n-Taa ga in-Satsu sa-re-Ma-sen.

I can't access my email.
電子メールにアクセスできません。
Den-shi me-Ru ni a-ku-se-su De-ki-ma-Sen.

I forgot my password.
パスワードを忘れました。
Pa-su-Waa-do wo wa-si-re-Ma-shi-ta.

The CD/DVD drive is not working.
CD/DVDドライブが動作していません。
Si-di-i/ di-i-vi-i-di-i do-rai-Bu ga do-o-sa-i-te i-Ma-se-n.

I'm having trouble with my [device or software].
[device or software] に問題があります。
[ ] ni mon-da-i Ga a-ri-ma-su.

Can you help me troubleshoot the issue?
問題のトラブルシューティングを手伝ってもらえますか？
Mon-da-i no to-ra-bu-ru-shuu-Tin-gu wo te-tsu-da-tte mo-rae-Ma-su
ka?

What should I do if my [device or software] isn't working properly?
[device or software] が正常に動作しない場合、どうすればよいで
すか？
[ ] ga se-i-jo-u ni do-o-sa-i si-na-i Ba-a-i, do-o Su-re-ba yo-i de-su Ka?

I'm getting an error message. What does it mean?
エラーメッセージが表示されます。どういう意味ですか？
e-Raa-me-se-ji-i ga hi-yo-u-sa-re-Ma-su.

How do I update my [device or software]?
[device or software] を更新する方法は何ですか？
[ ] o Koushin suru Houhou wa nan Desu ka?

Can you walk me through the steps to fix the problem?
問題を解決する手順を教えていただけますか？
Mondai o Kaiketsu Suru tejun o oshiete Itadakemasu ka?

How long will the repair take?
修理にどのくらい時間がかかりますか？
Shuuri ni Dono kurai jikan ga Kakarimasu ka?

Is it possible to recover lost data from my [device or software]?

[device or software] から失われたデータを回復することはできますか？

[ ] kara Ushinawareta deeta o Kaifuku suru koto wa Dekimasu ka?

# SMALL TALK

Hello, how are you?
こんにちは、お元気ですか？
Konnichiwa, o-genki desu ka?

How's it going?
調子はどうですか？
Choushi wa dou desu ka?

What have you been up to lately?
最近どうしてましたか？
Saikin dou Shitemashita ka?

How was your weekend?
週末はどうでしたか？
Shuumatsu wa dou Deshita ka?

Did you catch the game last night?
昨晩の試合を見ましたか？
Sakuban no shiai wo Mimashita ka?

What do you like to do in your free time?
自由時間に何をするのが好きですか？
Jiyuu jikan ni Nani wo Suru no ga Suki desu Ka?

How's work/school going?
仕事/学校はどうですか？
Shigoto/gakkou wa Dou desu ka?

Do you have any plans for the weekend?
週末の予定はありますか？
Shuumatsu no yotei Wa Arimasu ka?

What's new with you?
最近のあなたはどうですか？
Saikin no Anata wa dou Desu ka?

How's the family doing?
家族はお元気ですか？
Kazoku wa o-Genki desu ka?

What kind of music do you like?
んな音楽が好きですか？
Donna ongaku ga Suki desu ka?

Have you tried any new restaurants lately?
最近新しいレストランに行きましたか？
Saikin atarashii Resutoran ni Ikimashita ka?

What's your favorite hobby?
あなたの趣味は何ですか？
Anata no Shumi wa nan Desu ka?

Are you originally from around here?
ここ出身ですか？
koko Shusshin Desu ka?

What do you think about the weather today?
今日の天気はどう思いますか？
Kyou no Tenki wa dou Omoimasu ka?

Do you like to travel?
旅行が好きですか？
Ryokou ga Suki Desu ka?

Where have you been?
どこに行きましたか？
Doko ni Ikimashita ka?

Do you like to read?
読書が好きですか？
Dokusho ga Suki desu ka?

What's your favorite book?
あなたのお気に入りの本は何ですか？
Anata no okiniiri no Hon wa nan Desu ka?

What do you do for exercise?
運動は何をしますか？
Undou wa nani wo Shimasu ka?

Do you have any siblings?
兄弟はいますか？
Kyoudai wa Imasu ka?

Do you like to cook?
料理するのが好きですか？
Ryouri suru no Ga suki Desu ka?

What's your favorite kind of food?
あなたの好きな食べ物は何ですか？
Anata no suki na Tabemono wa nan Desu ka?

Do you have favorite places to visit?
訪れたい場所はありますか？
Otozuretai basho wa Arimasu ka?

What's your favorite season?
あなたの好きな季節は何ですか？
Anata no suki na Kisetsu wa nan Desu ka?

What's your favorite holiday?
あなたのお気に入りの休日は何ですか？
Anata no okiniiri no Kyuujitsu wa Nan Desu ka?

How was your weekend?
週末はどうでしたか？
Shuumatsu wa Dou Deshita ka?

What kind of music do you like?
あなたはどのような音楽が好きですか？
Anata wa Dono you na Ongaku ga suki Desu ka?

Do you have any travel plans coming up?
近々旅行の予定はありますか？
Chikajiku ryokou no Yotei wa Arimasu ka?

Have you tried any good restaurants in the area?
最近、良いレストランを試しましたか？
Saikin, yoi Resutoran wo Tameshimashita ka?

What are your favorite hobbies or activities to do in your free time?
あなたの好きな趣味や自由時間の過ごし方は何ですか？
Anata no suki na shumi ya jiyuu jikan no Sugoshi-kata wa nan Desu ka?

What's the best thing that's happened to you recently?
最近あった最高のことは何ですか？
Saikin atta saikou no Koto wa nan Desu ka?

Do you have any favorite Dutch traditions or festivals?
お気に入りのオランダの伝統や祭りはありますか？
Okiniiri no oranda no Dentou ya matsuri wa Arimasu ka?

What do you like about living/working in the Netherlands?
オランダでの生活・仕事で好きなことは何ですか？
Oranda de no seikatsu/shigoto De suki na Koto wa nan Desu ka?

Are you reading any good books or watching any good TV shows at the moment?
最近、良い本を読んでいますか？または、良いテレビ番組を見ていますか？
Saikin, yoi hon wo yonde Imasu ka? Matawa, yoi terebi Bangumi wo mite iMasu ka?

What are your hobbies or interests?
あなたの趣味や興味は何ですか？
Anata no shumi ya Kyoumi wa nan Desu ka?

Do you have any pets?
ペットは飼っていますか？
Petto wa katte Imasu ka?

What's your favorite Dutch food?
あなたのお気に入りのオランダ料理は何ですか？
Anata no okiniiri no Oranda ryouri wa Nan desu ka?

Do you have any plans for the upcoming holidays?
来る休日の計画はありますか？
Kuru kyuujitsu no Keikaku wa Arimasu ka?

Nice weather today, isn't it?
今日はいい天気ですね。
Kyou wa ii tenki Desu ne?

## ON A DATE

Hi, it's great to finally meet you!
こんにちは、ようやくお会いできて嬉しいです！
Konnichiwa, youyaku Oai dekite Ureshii desu!

Would you like a drink?
お飲み物はいかがですか？
Onnomimono wa Ikaga Desu ka?

What do you do for fun?
楽しいことは何をしますか？
Tanoshii koto wa Nani wo Shimasu ka?

Tell me about yourself.
自己紹介をお願いします。
Jikoshoukai wo Onegaishimasu

What kind of music do you like?
どんな音楽が好きですか？
Donna ongaku ga suki Desu ka?

What do you like to do in your free time?
暇なときに何をするのが好きですか？
Hima na toki ni nani wo Suru no ga suki Desu ka?

This place is really nice, don't you think?
ここはとても素敵な場所ですね、あなたもそう思いませんか？
Koko wa totemo Suteki na basho Desu ne, anata mo Sou Omoimasen ka?

So, how did you get into your line of work?
では、どのようにして今のお仕事に就くことになったのですか？
Dewa, dono you ni shite ima no Oshigoto ni tsuku koto ni Natta no Desu ka?

29

What's your favorite movie?
お気に入りの映画は何ですか？
Okiniiri no Eiga wa nan Desu ka?

Can I get your opinion on something?
何か意見を伺ってもいいですか？
Nanika iken wo Ukagatte mo ii Desu ka?

So, what brings you here tonight?
では、今晩は何のためにここに来たのですか？
Dewa, konban wa nan no Tame ni koko ni Kita no Desu ka?

What do you like to do for fun?
楽しいことは何をするのが好きですか？
Tanoshii koto wa nani wo Suru no ga suki Desu ka?

It's really nice to meet you.
お会いできてとても嬉しいです。
Oai dekite Totemo ureshii Desu

You look great tonight.
今晩は素晴らしいお姿ですね。
Konban wa Subarashii o-Sugata Sesu ne

This restaurant/bar/coffee shop is really nice.
このレストラン/バー/コーヒーショップは本当に素敵です。
Kono resutoran/ba-/kohi-Shoppu wa Hontou ni suteki Desu

Have you traveled to any interesting places lately?
最近、面白い場所に行きましたか？
Saikin, omoshiroi Basho ni Ikimashita ka?

What's your favorite Dutch food or restaurant?
お気に入りのオランダ料理やレストランは何ですか？
Okiniiri no Oranda ryouri ya resutoran wa nan Desu ka?

What do you think about [topic of conversation]?
[topic] についてどう思いますか？
[ ] ni tsuite dou Omoimasu ka?

What's the best date you've ever been on?
あなたが今までに行った中で最高のデートは何ですか？
Anata ga ima made ni itta Naka de saikou no Deeto wa nan Desu ka?

What is the best date you have ever been on?
あなたが今までに行った中で最高のデートは何ですか？
Anata ga ima made ni itta naka de Saikou no deeto wa nan Desu ka?

What kind of movies or TV shows do you enjoy watching?
どんな映画やテレビ番組が好きですか？
Donna eiga ya terebi Bangumi ga suki Desu ka?

What are your career goals or aspirations?
あなたのキャリアの目標や希望は何ですか？
Anata no kyaria no Mokuhyou ya kibou wa nan Desu ka?

Do you have any hobbies or interests?
趣味や興味がありますか？
Shumi ya Kyoumi ga Arimasu ka?

What are your favorite things to do in your free time?
あなたの自由時間に好きなことは何ですか？
Anata no jiyuu Jikan ni suki na Koto wa nan desu ka?

I'd love to see you again.
また会いたいです。
Mata aitai Desu.

# SHOPPING FOR CLOTHES

Do you have this item in a different color?
別の色はありますか？
Betsu no iro wa Arimasu ka?

How much is this?
これはいくらですか？
Kore wa Ikura Desu ka?

Is there a sale going on right now?
今セールをしていますか？
Ima se-ru o Shite Imasu ka?

Do you offer any discounts or promotions?
割引やプロモーションはありますか？
Waribiki ya Puromo-shon wa Arimasu ka?

Can I try this on?
これを試着してもいいですか？
Kore o shichaku Shite mo ii Desu ka?

Where are the fitting rooms located?
試着室はどこですか？
Shichakushitsu wa Doko desu ka?

How does this look on me?
これは私にどう見えますか？
Kore wa Watashi ni dou Miemasu ka?

Can you suggest any accessories to go with this?
これに合うアクセサリーをおすすめしていただけますか？
Kore ni au akusesarii o Osusume shite Itadakemasu ka?

What is your return policy?
返品についての規定は何ですか？
Henpin ni tsuite no Kitei wa nan Desu ka?

Do you have a gift receipt?
ギフトレシートはありますか？
Gifuto reshi-to wa Arimasu ka?

Is there an ATM nearby?
近くにATMはありますか？
Chikaku ni ei ti Emu wa Arimasu ka?

Can I have a receipt, please?
レシートをもらえますか？
Reshi-to o Moraemasu ka?

How much is the tax on this item?
この商品の税金はいくらですか？
Kono shouhin no Zeikin wa ikura Desu ka?

Is there a shipping fee for online orders?
オンライン注文に送料はかかりますか？
Onrain chuumon ni Souryo wa Kakarimasu ka?

Can I track my order online?
オンラインで注文状況を確認できますか？
Onrain de chuumon Joukyou wo kakunin Dekimasu ka?

Do you ship internationally?
海外への発送は可能ですか？
Kaigai e no hassou wa Kanou Desu ka?

Can I return the item by mail?
郵送で商品を返品できますか？
Yuusou de shouhin wo henpin Dekimasu ka?

Hello, I'm looking for [item of clothing].
[item] を探しています。
[ ] wo Sagashite imasu.

Do you have it in my size?
私のサイズはありますか？
Watashi no saizu wa Arimasu ka?

Can you help me find a [specific style/brand] of clothing?
[brand] の衣類を探すのを手伝っていただけますか？
[ ] no irui wo Sagasu no wo Tetsudatte itadakemasu ka?

What is your return policy?
返品についての規定は何ですか？
Henpin ni tsuite no Kitei wa nan Desu ka?

What is your return policy?
返品についての規定は何ですか？
Henpin ni Tsuite no kitei wa nan Desu ka?

May I try this on?
これを試着してもいいですか？
Kore wo Shichaku shite mo ii Desu ka?

How long does it take to process a return or exchange?
返品や交換の処理にはどのくらい時間がかかりますか？
Henpin ya koukan no Shori ni wa dono kurai Jikan ga kakarimasu

Do you offer any alterations or tailoring services?
お直しやお直しサービスはありますか？
Onaoshi ya onaoshi Saabisu wa arimasu ka?

Can I have this [item of clothing] gift wrapped?
この [item] をギフトラップしてもらえますか？
Kono [ ] o gifuto Rappu shite Moraemasu ka?

What is the shipping cost for this item?
この品物の送料はいくらですか？
Kono hinmono no Souryougo wa ikura Desu ka?

Do you offer free shipping for orders over a certain amount?
ある金額以上の注文には送料無料のサービスを提供していますか？
Aru kingaku ijou no Chuumon ni wa souryou Muryou no saabisu o Teikyou shite Imasu ka?

Can I track my shipment?
配送状況を追跡できますか？
Haisou joukyou o Tsuiseki dekimasu ka?

Do you have any recommendations for similar items that I might like?
似たような品物でおすすめのものはありますか？
Nita you na hinmono de Osusume no mono wa Arimasu ka?

# SIMPLE ANSWERS TO COMMON QUESTION

I'm doing well, thanks for asking. How about you?
わたしはげんきです。きいてくれてありがとう。あなたはどう
ですか？
Watashi wa genki desu. Kiite kurete arigatou. Anata wa dou desu ka?

My name is [name], nice to meet you.
わたしのなまえは [name] です。よろしくおねがいします。
Watashi no namae wa [ ] desu. Yoroshiku onegaishimasu.

I'm from [country/city], how about you?
わたしは [country/city] からきました。あなたはどこからきまし
たか？
Watashi wa [ ] kara kimashita. Anata wa doko kara kimashita ka?

I work as a [occupation], what about you?
わたしは [occupation] としてはたらいています。あなたはどん
なしごとをしていますか？
Watashi wa [ ] toshite hataraitte imasu. Anata wa donna shigoto wo
shite imasu ka?

I enjoy [activity/hobby], how about you?
わたしは [activity/hobby] をするのがすきです。あなたはどんな
ことがすきですか？
Watashi wa [ ] wo suru no ga suki desu. Anata wa donna koto ga suki
desu ka?

Can I help you with anything?
なにかてつだいができますか？
Nanika tetsudai ga dekimasu ka?

## ASKING FOR AND GIVING DIRECTIONS

*Insert the destination where applicable

Excuse me, can you tell me how to get to [destination]?
すみません、[destination] への行き方を教えていただけますか？
Sumimasen, [ ] e no ikikata wo Oshiete Itadakemasu ka?

Could you help me find my way to _____?
までの行き方を教えていただけますか？
Made no Ikikata wo oshiete Itadakemasu ka?

Do you know how I can get to _____?
に行くにはどうすればいいですか？
Ni i iku ni wa dou Sureba ii Desu ka?

Which way is _____?
はどちらにありますか？
Wa Dochira ni Arimasu ka?

Can you give me directions to _____?
までの道案内をしていただけますか？
Made no michiannai wo Shite Itadakemasu ka?

I'm lost.
道に迷ってしまいました。
Michi ni mayotte Shimaimashita.

Can you tell me how to get to _____?
までの行き方を教えていただけますか？
Made no ikikata wo Oshiete itadakemasu ka?

I'm trying to find _____, can you point me in the right direction?
を探しているのですが、正しい方向を教えていただけますか？
Wo sagashite iru no desu ga, Tadashii houkou wo Oshiete itadakemasu ka?

Can you tell me how far _____ is from here?
ここから_____までどのくらいの距離がありますか？
Koko kara _____ made Dono kurai no Kyori ga Arimasu ka?

Is it far from here to _____?
ここから_____まで遠いですか？
Koko kara _____ made Tooi desu ka?

Go straight ahead.
まっすぐ進んでください。
Massugu susunde kudasai.

Turn left/right at the next corner.
次の角を左/右に曲がってください。
Tsugi no Kado wo hidari/migi ni Magatte kudasai.

Cross the street.
道路を渡ってください。
Douro wo watatte Kudasai.

Go past the _____ on your left/right.
左/右にある_____を通り過ぎてください。
Hidari/migi ni aru _____ wo Toorisugite kudasai.

It's on your left/right.
は左/右側にあります。
Wa hidari/migi Gawa ni Arimasu.

I'm a bit lost, could you please help me find my way to [destination]?
少し道に迷ってしまいました。[destination] までの行き方を教え
ていただけませんか？
Sukoshi michi ni mayotte Shimaimashita. [ ] made no ikikata wo
Oshiete itadakemasen ka?

Do you know where [street/landmark] is located?
[Street/landmark] はどこにありますか？
[ ] wa Doko ni Arimasu ka?

Can you give me directions to [destination]?
[Destination] への行き方を教えていただけますか？
[ ] e no Ikikata wo oshiete Itadakemasu ka?

# COMMON BUSINESS STATEMENTS AND QUESTIONS

What is the purpose of this meeting?
このミーティングの目的は何ですか？
Kono meeting no Mokuteki wa nan Desu ka?

Can you give me an update on the progress?
進捗状況を教えていただけますか？
Shinchoku jyokyo wo Oshiete Itadakemasu ka?

How can I improve my sales?
売上をどうやって改善（かいぜん）できますか？
Uriae wo dou yatte Kaizen Dekimasu ka?

What are our strengths and weaknesses?
私たちの強みと弱みは何ですか？
Watashitachi no Tsuyomi to jakumi wa nan Desu ka?

Can you explain the process?
プロセスについて説明していただけますか？
Process ni tsuite Setsumei shite Itadakemasu ka?

What is the timeline for this project?
このプロジェクトのスケジュールは何ですか？
Kono project no Schedule wa nan Desu ka?

What are the deliverables for this project?
このプロジェクトの成果物は何ですか？
Kono project no Seikamono wa nan Desu ka?

How can we streamline the process?
プロセスをどうやって効率化（こうりつか）できますか？
Process wo dou yatte Kouritsuka Dekimasu ka?

Can you provide more information?
もっと詳しい情報を提供していただけますか？
Motto kuwashii Joho wo teikyou Shite Itadakemasu ka?

What is the target audience?
ターゲットオーディエンスは何ですか？
Target audience wa nan Desu ka?

Wat is de doelgroep?
は何ですか？
Doelgroep wa nan Desu ka?

How can we cut costs?
コストを削減する方法はありますか？
Kosuto wo sakugen Suru houhou wa Arimasu ka?

What are the risks involved?
どのようなリスクがあるのでしょうか？
Dono youna Risuku ga aru no Deshou ka?

What are the project milestones?
プロジェクトのマイルストーンは何ですか？
Purojekuto no Mairusutoon wa nan Desu ka?

What is the target completion date?
目標の完成日はいつですか？
Mokuhyou no Kanseibi wa itsu desu ka?

Thank you for your email.
メールをありがとうございます。
Meeru wo Arigatou gozaimasu.

I'm writing to follow up on our previous conversation.
前回の会話の続きを書いています。
Zenkai no kaiwa no Tsuzuki wo kaite Imasu.

We appreciate your interest in our company.
弊社に興味を持っていただきありがとうございます。
Heisha ni kyoumi wo Motte itadaki Arigatou gozaimasu.

Our team is currently working on [project/task].
弊社のチームは現在[project/task]に取り組んでいます。
Heisha no chiimu wa Genzai [project/task] ni torikunde Imasu.

We'd like to schedule a meeting to discuss [topic].
[topic] について話し合うためにミーティングを予定したいと思います。
Topic ni tsuite hanashiau Tame ni miitingu wo Yotei shitai to Omoimasu.

Can you provide more details on [topic]?
[topic] についてもっと詳細を教えていただけますか？
Topic ni tsuite motto Shousai wo oshiete Itadakemasu ka?

What's the timeline for this task?
タスクのタイムラインは何ですか？
Tasuku no Taimurain wa nan Desu ka?

Do you have any questions or concerns about the proposal?
提案について何かご質問やご心配な点はありますか？
Teian ni tsuite nanika go Shitsumon ya go Shinpai na ten wa Arimasu ka?

What's your budget for this project/task?
このプロジェクト/タスクの予算はいくらですか？
Kono purojekuto/tasuku no Yosan wa ikura Desu ka?

When is the best time for us to schedule a meeting?
ミーティングの予定を決めるのに最適な時間はいつですか？
Miitingu no yotei wo Kimeru no ni saiteki na

# STAYING AT A HOTEL

What time is check-in/check-out?
チェックイン/チェックアウトは何時ですか？
chekku-in/chekku-Auto wa nan-ji Desu ka?

Is there a restaurant on-site?
敷地内にレストランはありますか？
Shikichinai ni Resutoran wa Arimasu ka?

Is breakfast included in my room rate?
朝食は部屋代に含まれていますか？
Choushoku wa heya-dai ni Fukumarete Imasu ka?

Is there a shuttle service to the airport/train station?
空港や駅へのシャトルサービスはありますか？
Kuukou ya eki e no shatoru Saabisu wa arimasu ka?

Can I get a late check-out?
レイトチェックアウトはできますか？
Reito chekku Auto wa Dekimasu ka?

Do you offer room service?
ルームサービスはありますか？
Ruumu saabisu wa Arimasu ka?

Is there a pool?
プールはありますか？
Puuru wa Arimasu ka?

Is there a laundry service available?
ランドリーサービスはありますか？
Randori- saabisu wa Arimasu ka?

Is there a safe in the room?
部屋にセーフティボックスはありますか？
Heya ni seefuti Bkkusu wa Arimasu ka?

Can you recommend a good local restaurant?
地元のおいしいレストランをおすすめしていただけますか？
Jimoto no oishii resutoran o Osusume shite Itadakemasu ka?

Is there a mini-bar in the room?
部屋にミニバーはありますか？
Heya ni mini ba- wa Arimasu ka?

Do you have any rooms available for [date]?
[date] に空き部屋はありますか？
[ ] ni aki Heya wa Arimasu ka?

Is breakfast included in the room rate?
部屋料金に朝食は含まれていますか？
Heya ryokan ni Choushoku wa Fukumarete imasu ka?

Can you provide me with a map of the area?
地図を提供していただけますか？
Chizu o teikyou shite Itadakemasu ka?

What time is checkout?
チェックアウトは何時ですか？
Chekku auto wa nan-ji Desu ka?

Can I have some extra towels and toiletries?
タオルやアメニティを追加で提供していただけますか？
Taoru ya ameniti o Tsuika de teikyou Shite itadakemasu ka?

Is there a restaurant or café on-site?
敷地内にレストランやカフェはありますか？
Shikichinai ni resutoran ya Kafe wa Arimasu ka?

Do you offer any tours or activities in the area?
エリア内でツアーやアクティビティを提供していますか？
Eria nai de tsua- ya Akutibiti o teikyou Shite imasu ka?

44

Can I get a discount if I book for a longer period of time?

長期滞在の場合に割引がありますか？

Chouki taizai no Baai ni waribiki ga Arimasu ka?

# WEATHER

What's the weather like today?
今日の天気はどうですか？
Kyou no tenki wa dou Desu ka?

Is it supposed to rain/snow later?
後で雨/雪が降る予定ですか？
Ato de ame/yuki ga Furu yotei Desu ka?

What's the temperature right now?
現在の気温は何度ですか？
Genzai no kion wa nando Desu ka?

Is it hot outside?
外は暑いですか？
Soto wa atsui Desu ka?

Is it cold outside?
外は寒いですか？
Soto wa samui Desu ka?

What's the temperature?
気温は何度ですか？
Kion wa nando Desu ka?

Will it be sunny tomorrow?
明日は晴れる予定ですか？
Ashita wa hareru Yotei Desu ka?

Is there a chance of thunderstorms?
雷雨の可能性はありますか？
Raiu no kanousei wa Arimasu ka?

Is it going to snow?
雪が降る予定ですか？
Yuki ga furu Yotei Desu ka?

What's the forecast for tomorrow?
明日の予報は何ですか？
Ashita no Yohou wa nan Desu ka?

Is it windy outside?
外は風が強いですか？
Soto wa kaze ga Tsuyoi Desu ka?

What's the humidity like?
湿度はどうですか？
Shitsudo wa Dou Desu ka?

Is it foggy outside?
外は霧がかかっていますか？
Soto wa kiri ga Kakatte Imasu ka?

Will it be clear tonight?
今夜は晴れる予定ですか？
Kon'ya wa hareru Yotei Desu ka?

Is it going to be humid?
蒸し暑くなる予定ですか？
Mushiatsuku naru yotei Desu ka?

What's the chance of precipitation?
降水確率はどのくらいですか？
Kousui kakuritsu wa dono Kurai Desu ka?

How hot does it get here in the summer?
夏になるとどのくらい暑くなりますか？
Natsu ni naru to dono Kurai atsuku Narimasu ka?

How cold does it get here in the winter?
冬になるとどのくらい寒くなりますか？
Fuyu ni naru to dono Kurai samuku Narimasu ka?

Is there a hurricane coming?
ハリケーンが来る予定ですか？
Harikuen ga Kuru yotei Desu ka?

What is the UV index?
UVインデックスは何ですか？
Yuu-vii in-Dek-kusu wa nan Desu ka?

Are there any weather warnings?
天気警報はありますか？
Ten-ki kei-hou wa Ari masu ka?

Have areas been affected by flooding?
洪水による被害はありましたか？
Kou-zui ni yoru hi-Gai wa ari Mashi ta ka?

Is it safe to travel in this weather?
この天気で旅行するのは安全ですか？
Ko-no ten-ki de ryokou Suru no wa an-zen Desu ka?

Will the weather affect my flight?
天気がフライトに影響しますか？
Ten-ki ga fu-rai-to ni Eikyou shi Masu ka?

Do you know what the forecast is for tomorrow?
明日の天気予報を知っていますか？
Ashita no ten-ki Yohou o shi tte i Masu ka?

Are there any weather warnings or alerts in effect?
天気警報や注意報は出ていますか？
Ten-ki kei-hou ya chuui-hou wa de te i Masu ka?

It's a beautiful day outside.
外は素晴らしい日です。
Soto wa subarashii hi Desu.

I love when it rains.
雨が降るととてもリラックスします。
ame ga furu to totemo rirakkusu shimasu.

It's so relaxing.
とてもリラックスします。
totemo rirakkusu shimasu.

# AT THE HOSPITAL

What tests do I need to undergo?
必要な検査は何ですか？
Hitsuyou na Kensa wa Nanidesu ka?

Do you need me to fast before any tests?
検査前に断食する必要がありますか？
Kensa mae ni danshoku suru Hitsuyou ga Arimasu ka?

How long will it take to get the test results?
検査結果が出るまでにどのくらい時間がかかりますか？
Kensa kekka ga deru made ni Dono kurai jikan ga Kakarimasu ka?

What is the diagnosis?
診断結果は何ですか？
Shindan Kekka wa Nanidesu ka?

What is the cause of my symptoms?
私の症状の原因は何ですか？
Watashi no Shoujou no gen'in wa Nanidesu ka?

Is the condition serious?
病状は深刻ですか？
Byoujou wa Shinkoku Desu ka?

What are my treatment options?
私の治療オプションは何ですか？
Watashi no chiryou Opushon wa Nanidesu ka?

What is causing my symptoms?
私の症状を引き起こしている原因は何ですか？
Watashi no Shoujou o hikiokoshiteiru gen'in wa Nanidesu ka?

What tests, if any, do I need to have done?
必要ならば、どのような検査を受ける必要がありますか？
Hitsuyou naraba, donoyouna Kensa wo ukeru Hitsuyou ga Arimasu ka?

How long will it take for the treatment to work?
治療が効果を発揮するのにどのくらい時間がかかりますか？
Chiryou ga kouka wo Hakkitsu suru no ni dono Kurai jikan ga Kakarimasu ka?

How long do I need to take the medication or treatment?
薬や治療をどのくらいの期間摂取する必要がありますか？
Kusuri ya Chiryou wo dono Kurai no kikan Sesshu suru hitsuyou ga Arimasu ka?

Can you explain the benefits and risks of each treatment option?
各治療オプションの利点とリスクを説明していただけますか？
Kaku chiryou o Pushon no riten to Risuku wo setsumei Shite itadakemasu ka?

What are the side effects of the medications you are prescribing?
処方している薬の副作用は何ですか？
Shohoushite iru Kusuri no Fukusayou wa Nanidesu ka?

Can I continue with my current medications?
現在の薬を続けても大丈夫ですか？
geNzai no KU-ru yen wo tSU-zu-ke-te mo dai-JO-bu desu ka?

Can I stop taking the medication once the symptoms subside?
症状が軽くなれば、薬をやめてもいいですか？
SHO-jo ga ka-ru-ku na-re-ba, KU-ru wo ya-me-te mo ii desu ka?

How often should I come for a follow-up appointment?
再診の予約はどのくらいの頻度で取るべきですか？
Sai-shin no yo-Yaku wa do-no-ku-rai no hin-do de to-ru Be-ki desu ka?

Is there anything I can do to manage my symptoms at home?
自宅で症状を管理する方法はありますか？
TAKU de SHO-jo wo kan-ri su-Ru ho-ho wa a-ri-Masu ka?

What lifestyle changes do I need to make to improve my health?

健康を改善するためにどのような生活習慣の変化が必要ですか？

ken-KO wo ka-i-zen su-ru ta-me-ni do-no yo-u-na se-i-Katsu shu-kan no hen-ka ga hi-Tsu-yo Desu ka?

Can you recommend any specialists if needed?

必要に応じて、専門家をお勧めいただけますか？

Hitsu-yo ni o-u-ji-te, sen-Mon-ka wo o-su-se-me i-ta-da-ke-Mas-ka?

Can you write me a prescription for this medication?

この薬の処方箋を書いていただけますか？

Ko-no ku-ru no sho-ho-Sen wo ka-i-te i-Ta-da-ke-mas-ka?

How long should I rest after the procedure?

手順の後、どのくらい休息すべきですか？

Te-jun no ato, do-no-ku-rai kyu-u-Soku su-be-ki desu ka?

What is the best way to manage pain?

痛みの管理の最善策は何ですか？

Itami no kanri no Saizensaku wa Nanidesu ka?

Can I take over-the-counter medications with this prescription?

この処方箋と一緒に市販薬を服用しても良いですか？

Kono shohousen to issho ni shi han-yaku o Fukuyou shite mo yoi Desu ka?

Can you tell me more about my diagnosis/treatment options?

自分の診断/治療オプションについてもっと教えてもらえますか？

Jibun no shindan/chiryou Opushon ni tsuite Motto oshiete Moraemasu ka?

How long will I need to stay in the hospital/recovery from this procedure?
この手続きからの入院/回復にはどのくらいの期間が必要ですか？
Kono tetsuzuki Kara no nyuuin/kaifuku ni wa Dono kurai no kikan ga Hitsuyou desu ka?

Do I need to make any changes to my medication/diet/lifestyle to manage my condition?
私の状態を管理するために、私は私の薬/食事/ライフスタイルに何か変更する必要がありますか？
Watashi no joutai o kanri suru tame ni, Watashi wa watashi no kusuri/shokuzi/raifusutairu ni Nanika henkou Suru hitsuyou ga Arimasu ka?

Can you explain the billing/insurance process for my visit/procedure?
私の訪問/手続きの請求/保険手続きについて説明していただけますか？
Watashi no houmon/tetsuzuki no Seikyu/hoken Tetsuzuki ni tsuite Setsumei shite Itadakemasu ka?

When is the next available appointment with the doctor?
次に利用可能な医師の予約はいつですか？
Tsugi ni riyou kanou na ishi no Yoyaku wa itsu Desu ka?

I would like to schedule an appointment with the doctor.
医者に予約をしたいです。
Isha ni yoyaku wo Shitai desu.

I'm feeling quite unwell.
体調があまり良くありません。
Taichou ga Amari yoku Arimasen.

I need a check-up.
健康診断が必要です。
kenkou shindan ga Hitsuyou Desu.

I have some concerns about my health.
健康について心配があります。
kenkou ni Tsuite shinpai ga Arimasu.

I've been experiencing some pain in my [body part].
[身体の部位]に痛みを感じています。
[Shintai no bui] ni Itami wo Kanjiteimasu.

I need a referral to see a specialist.
専門医を受診するための紹介状が必要です。
Senmon-i wo jushin suru Tame no shoukaijou ga Hitsuyou desu.

I'm here for a follow-up appointment.
再診のために来ました。
Saishin no Tame ni Kimashita.

I'm here for a second opinion.
セカンドオピニオンを受けるために来ました。
Sekando opinion wo Ukeru tame ni Kimashita.

I need to renew my prescription.
処方箋を更新する必要があります。
Shohousen wo Koushin suru Hitsuyou ga Arimasu.

I'm allergic to [medication] and need to avoid it.
[medication] にアレルギーがあり、避ける必要があります。
[ ] ni Arerugii ga ari, yokeru Hitsuyou ga Arimasu.

I've been feeling tired and rundown lately.
最近、疲れやすく、体調が優れないです。
Saikin, tsukareyasuku, Taichou ga yosorenai Desu.

I need to discuss my test results with the doctor.
医者と検査結果について話したいです。
i-sha to ken-sa Kek-ka ni tsu-i-te ha-na-Shi-tai desu.

I'm having trouble sleeping.
眠れない悩みがあります。
Ne-mu-re-nai na-yo-Mi ga a-ri-Masu.

I need a flu shot or other vaccine.
インフルエンザの予防接種が必要です。
In-fu-ru-en-za no yo-bo-u Set-su ga hi-tsu-yo-u Desu.

I'm pregnant and need to discuss my prenatal care.
妊娠中で、出産前のケアについて話したいです。
Nin-shin-chuu de, shu-san-Mae no ke-a ni tsu-i-te ha-na-Shi-tai desu.

I've been experiencing some side effects from my medication.
薬の副作用が出ています。
Ku-su-ri no Fu-ku-sa-yo-u Ga de-te i-Masu.

I need a physical exam.
身体検査が必要です。
Shin-tai ken-sa ga hi-Tsu-yo-u Desu.

I need a note for work or school.
仕事や学校のための診断書が必要です。
Shi-go-to ya ga-ku-ko no ta-me no Shin-dan-sho ga hi-Tsu-yo-u Desu.

I need to discuss my diet and nutrition with the doctor.
医者と食事と栄養について話したいです。
i-Sha to shoku-ji to ei-yo-u ni Tsu-i-te ha-na-shi-tai Desu.

I need to have my blood pressure checked.
血圧を測定してもらいたいです。
Ke-tsu-atsu o sok-tei shi-te Mo-rai-tai Desu.

I have a cough or sore throat.
私は風邪やのどが痛いです。
Wa-ta-shi wa ka-ze ya no-do ga i-Tai desu.

I have a fever or other flu-like symptoms.
私は熱があります、または体温のような症状があります。
Wa-ta-shi wa ne-tsu ga a-ri-ma-su, Ma-ta-ha ta-i-fu no yo-u na
Shou-jou ga a-ri-Ma-su.

I need a prescription for a medication.
薬の処方箋が必要です。
Ku-su-ri no sho-ho-u-sen ga hi-Tsu-you Desu.

I have an appointment with the doctor.
医師との予約があります。
i-shi-Tsu no yo-Yaku ga a-ri-ma-su.

# WORKING OUT AT A GYM

What are the gym hours?
ジムの営業時間は何時から何時ですか？
Jimu no Eigyou jikan wa Nanji kara nanji Desu ka?

Do you have any classes today?
今日はクラスありますか？
Kyou wa Kurasu Arimasu ka?

Can I get a tour of the gym?
ジムの見学をすることはできますか？
Jimu no kengaku wo Suru koto wa Dekimasu ka?

Where are the lockers located?
ロッカーはどこにありますか？
Rokkaa wa doko ni Arimasu ka?

How much does it cost to use the gym?
ジムを利用するにはいくらかかりますか？
Jimu wo riyou Suru ni wa ikura Kakarimasu ka?

Can I borrow a towel?
タオルを借りることはできますか？
Taoru wo kariru Koto wa Dekimasu ka?

Where is the water fountain?
水飲み場はどこですか？
Mizu nomiba wa Doko desu ka?

Do you have any yoga mats?
ヨガマットはありますか？
Yogan matto wa Arimasu ka?

Is there a sauna here?
サウナはありますか？
Sauna wa Arimasu ka?

How do I use this machine?
この機械はどう使うんですか？
Kono kikai wa Dou tsukau n Desu ka?

Can you spot me?
スポットをしてくれますか？
Supotto wo Shite Kuremasu ka?

Where can I find the dumbbells?
ダンベルはどこにありますか？
Danberu wa Doko ni Arimasu ka?

Is there a locker room here?
更衣室はありますか？
Kouishitsu wa Arimasu ka?

How much does a personal trainer cost?
パーソナルトレーナーはいくらですか？
Paasonaru torenaa wa Ikura Desu ka?

Can I use the treadmill?
ランニングマシンを使ってもいいですか？
Ran'ningu mashin wo Tsukatte mo ii Desu ka?

Is there a weight limit on the machines?
このマシンに重量制限はありますか？
Kono mashin ni Juuryou seigen wa Arimasu ka?

Can I pay with a credit card?
クレジットカードで支払えますか？
kurejitto kaado de Haraebaemasu ka?

Where can I find the exercise balls?
エクササイズボールはどこにありますか？
Ekusasaizu booru wa Doko ni Arimasu ka?

How many reps and sets should I do?
何回セットをすればいいですか？
Nankai setto wo Sureba ii Desu ka?

Do you offer group classes?
グループレッスンはありますか？
Guruupu ressun wa Arimasu ka?

Can I bring a friend to the gym?
友達をジムに連れて行ってもいいですか？
Tomodachi wo Jimu ni tsurete itte mo ii Desu ka?

Is there a pool here?
プールはありますか？
Puuru wa Arimasu ka?

What kind of workouts are you doing today?
今日はどんなトレーニングをしていますか？
Kyou wa donna Toreningu wo shite Imasu ka?

Do you have any advice on how to improve my form for this exercise?
このエクササイズのフォームを改善するアドバイスがあります
か？
Kono ekusasaizu no Fo-mu wo Kaizen suru adobaisu ga Arimasu ka?

How many sets/reps are you doing for that exercise?
そのエクササイズは何セット/何回行いますか？
Sono ekusasaizu wa Nan setto/nan kai Okonaimasu ka?

Would you like to work in with me on this equipment?
この機材を一緒に使いませんか？
Kono kizai wo Issho ni Tsukaimasen ka?

Do you know how to use this piece of equipment?
この機材の使い方を知っていますか？
Kono kizai no Tsukaikata wo Shitte imasu ka?

This exercise is really challenging, but I'm going to push through it.
このエクササイズは本当にハードですが、がんばってやり遂げます。
Kono ekusasaizu wa Hontou ni haado desu ga, Ganbatte Yaritogemasu.

I like to switch up my workouts to keep things interesting.
興味を持続させるために、トレーニング内容を変えるのが好きです。
Kyoumi wo jizoku saseru tame ni, Toreningu naiyou wo Kaeru no ga Suki desu

# COMMON GREETINGS

Hello
こんにちは
Konnichiwa

Hi/Hey
やあ、こんにちは、もしもし
yaa, Konnichiwa, Moshi moshi

Good morning
おはようございます
Ohayou Gozaimasu

Good afternoon
こんにちは
Konnichiwa

Good evening
こんばんは
Konbanwa

Greetings
ご挨拶
Goaisatsu

What's up?
どうだい？
Dou dai?

How's it going?
調子はどうですか？
Choushi wa dou Desu ka?

How are you doing?
お元気ですか？
Ogenki Desu ka?

Nice to meet you
はじめまして
Hajimemashite

Pleasure to meet you
お会いできて光栄です
Oaidekite kouei Desu

It's good to see you
お会いできて嬉しいです
Oaidekite ureshii Desu

Long time no see
久しぶりですね
Hisashiburi Desu ne

Hey, what's going on with you today?
こんにちは、今日はどうですか？
konnichiwa, Kyou wa dou Desu ka?

Hi, how's your day going so far?
やあ、今日はどうですか？
Yaa, kyou wa dou Desu ka?

Good evening, how can I assist you?
こんばんは、どうかお力になれますか？
 KON-ban-wa, Dou ka o-Tsu-ka-ni na-re-ma-Su ka?

Good morning, how are you?
おはようございます、お元気ですか？
O-ha-yo-u go-Za-i-ma-su, o-Ge-nki de-Su ka?

Nice to see you again.
またお会いできてうれしいです。
Ma-ta o-ai-de-Ki-te u-re-shii De-su.

How have you been?
お元気ですか？最近どうですか？
O-ge-nki de-su ka? Sai-kin Dou de-su ka?

What's new?
最近どうですか？
Sai-kin dou De-su ka?

Hey there, how's it going?
こんにちは、調子はどうですか？
Kon-ni-chi-wa, Cho-u-shi Wa dou de-su ka?

Hey there, nice to see you!
こんにちは、お会いできてうれしいです！
Kon-ni-Chi-wa, o-ai-de-Ki-te u-re-shii De-su!

How's your day going so far?
今日はどうでしたか？
Kyo-u wa Dou de-shi-Ta ka?

What brings you here today?
今日は何の用事ですか？
Kyo-u wa Nan no yo-u-ji De-su ka?

I hope you're doing well.
お元気であれば幸いです。
O-ge-nki de a-re-Ba sa-i-wa-i De-su.

Hello, it's great to meet you!
こんにちは、お会いできて光栄です！
Kon-ni-chi-wa, o-ai-De-ki-te ko-u-ei De-su!

# BANKING

What types of bank accounts do you offer?
銀行口座にはどの種類がありますか？
Ginkou Kouza ni wa dono Shurui ga arimasu ka?

What are the requirements for opening a bank account?
銀行口座を開設するには、どのような条件がありますか？
Ginkou Kouza wo kaisetsu suru ni wa, Dono you na jouken ga Arimasu ka?

How do I transfer money to another account?
他の口座にお金を送金するにはどうすればいいですか？
Hoka no Kouza ni okane wo Soukin suru ni wa dou Sureba ii desu ka?

What are the fees for using your services?
サービス利用の手数料はどのくらいですか？
Saabisu riyou no Tesuuryou wa Dono kurai Desu ka?

Can I apply for a loan or credit card through your bank?
ローンやクレジットカードの申し込みは、貴行でできますか？
Roon ya kurejitto kaado no Moushikomi wa, koukou de Dekimasu ka?

How can I check my account balance?
口座残高はどうやって確認すればいいですか？
Kouza zandaka wa Dou yatte Kakunin Sureba ii Desu ka?

What happens if I lose my ATM card or it gets stolen?
ATMカードを紛失または盗まれた場合はどうなりますか？
ATM kaado wo Funshitsu matawa Nusumareta baai wa dou Narimasu ka?

Can I access my account online or through a mobile app?
アカウントにオンラインまたはモバイルアプリからアクセスできますか？
Akaunto ni Onrain Matawa mobairu Apuri kara akusesu Dekimasu ka?

64

# COMMON TRAVELER QUESTIONS

What are the visa requirements for visiting this country?
この国を訪れるためのビザ要件は何ですか？
Ko-no kuni o otozure-ru ta-me no BI-ZA yo-u-ken wa na-ni de-su ka?

What is the local emergency phone number?
緊急時の地域の電話番号は何ですか？
Kinkyuu-ji no chiiki no den-wa ban-go wa na-ni de-su ka?

Can I use my credit card here?
ここでクレジットカードを使えますか？
Ko-ko de KU-RE-JITTO KA-DO o tsu-ka-e-ma-su ka?

What is the public transportation system like?
公共交通機関はどのようなものですか？
Ko-kyou Kou-tsu ki-kan Wa do-no yo-u-na Mo-no de-su ka?

How do I navigate the local transportation system?
地元の交通システムをどのように移動しますか？
Ji-moto no kou-tsu Shi-sute-mu o do-no yo-u-ni i-do-u Shi-ma-Su ka?

Where can I find a pharmacy?
薬局はどこにありますか？
Yaku-kyoku Wa do-ko ni a-ri-Ma-su ka?

What is the local dress code?
地元のドレスコードは何ですか？
Ji-moto no DO-RESU KO-DO wa na-ni de-su ka?

Are there any areas I should avoid for safety reasons?
安全上避けるべきエリアはありますか？
An-zen jou sa-keru be-ki E-RI-A wa a-ri-ma-su ka?

What is the local time zone?
地元のタイムゾーンは何ですか？
Ji-moto no TAIMU ZO-N wa na-ni de-su ka?

How do I convert between currencies?
通貨をどのように変換しますか？
Tsuu-ka o do-no yo-u-ni he-n-kan shi-ma-su ka?

Where can I find public restrooms?
公衆トイレはどこにありますか？
Kou-shuu TOI-RE Wa do-ko ni a-ri-ma-Su ka?

How do I get to the airport/train station/bus station?
空港/駅/バスターミナルへの行き方はどうですか？
Kuu-ko-u / e-ki / ba-su-Ta-mi-na-ru e no i-ki-ka-ta wa Dou de-su ka?

What are some popular tourist attractions in this area?
このエリアで人気の観光スポットは何ですか？
 Ko-no e-ri-a De nin-ki no Kan-ko-u su-po-tto wa Nan de-su ka?

How much does this cost?
これはいくらですか？
Ko-re wa i-ku-ra De-su ka?

Can I drink the tap water here?
ここで蛇口の水を飲んでもいいですか？
Ko-ko de jagu-Chi no Mi-zu o non-de mo ii De-su ka?

What is the exchange rate for my currency?
私の通貨の為替レートは何ですか？
Wa-ta-shi no Tsuu-ka no ka-Wa-se ree-to wa nan De-su ka?

What is the local currency and exchange rate?
地元の通貨と為替レートは何ですか？
Chi-mo-to no Tsuu-ka to Ka-wa-se ree-to Wa nan de-su ka?

Where can I buy a SIM card for my phone?
スマートフォン用のSIMカードはどこで買えますか？
Su-ma-to-foon you no SIM ka-do wa do-ko de Kae-ma-su ka?

How do I ask for directions?
道を聞くにはどうすればいいですか？
Mi-chi o ki-ku ni wa dou su-re-ba ii de-su ka?

How do I call a taxi?
タクシーを呼ぶにはどうすればいいですか？
Tak-shii o yo-Bu ni wa dou Su-re-ba ii De-su ka?

Definitely not.
絶対にそうではありません。
Zettai ni sou de wa Arimasen.

Possibly
可能性があります
Kanousei ga Arimasu.

That's a Tough one.
それは難しい質問です
Sore wa Muzukashii shitsumon Desu.

I can see both sides of the argument.
議論の両面がわかります。
Giron no Ryoumen Ga wakarimasu.

It's hard to say for sure.
確実に言えることではありません。
Kakujitsu ni ieru Koto de wa Arimasen.

I'm inclined to agree/disagree with you.
私はあなたに同意/反対する傾向があります。
Watashi wa anata ni Doui/hantai suru keikou ga Arimasu.

What are the must-see attractions in this area?
このエリアで見逃せない観光スポットは何ですか？
Ko-no e-ri-a De mi-noga-se-nai Kan-ko-u su-po-tto wa Nan de-su ka?

How do I get to the airport/train station/bus terminal from here?
ここから空港/駅/バスターミナルに行くにはどうしたらいいです
か？
Kokokara kuukou/eki/basutaminaru ni Iku ni wa dou Shitara ii desu ka?

Can you recommend any good restaurants or cafes nearby?
近くに良いレストランやカフェをおすすめできますか？
Chikaku ni yoi resutoran ya Kafe o osusume Dekimasu ka?

How do I get around the city/town/area?
この市/町/地域をどうやって移動すればいいですか？
Kono shi/machi/chiiki wo dou Yatte idou sureba ii Desu ka?

What is the weather like during this time of year?
この時期の天気はどうですか？
Kono jiki no Tenki wa dou Desu ka?

Are there any safety concerns or areas to avoid in this location?
この場所で安全上の問題や避けた方が良い場所はありますか？
Kono basho de anzenjou no Mondai ya saketa hou ga yoi Basho wa
Arimasu ka?

How do I access Wi-Fi or mobile data in this area?
この地域でWi-Fiやモバイルデータにアクセスするにはどうした
らいいですか？
Kono chiiki de Wi-Fi ya mobairu Deeta ni akusesu Suru ni wa dou
Shitara ii Desu ka?

What are the local laws and regulations, such as visa requirements or
alcohol restrictions?
ビザ要件やアルコール規制など、地方の法律や規則は何ですか
？
Biza youken ya arukooru Kisei nado, chihou no Houritsu ya kisoku wa
Nan desu ka?

# COMMON RESPONSES TO QUESTIONS

Yes, that's correct.
はい、それは正しいです。
HAI, sore wa Tadashii Desu.

No, that's not accurate.
いいえ、それは正確ではありません。
IIE, sore wa Seikaku de wa Arimasen.

I'm not sure, let me check and get back to you.
わかりません、確認してからお返事します。
Wakarimasen, kakunin Shite kara ohenji Shimasu.

Sorry, I didn't understand your question.
すみません、質問が理解できませんでした。
Sumimasen, shitsumon Ga rikai Dekimasen deshita.

To be honest, I don't have an answer for that.
正直に言って、それについて答えがありません。
Shoujiki ni itte, Sore ni Tsuite Kotae ga arimasen.

That's a great question, let me think about it for a moment.
それは素晴らしい質問です。少し考えさせてください。
Sore wa subarashii Shitsumon desu. Sukoshi kangae sasete kudasai.

I'm afraid I don't know.
残念ですが、私は知りません。
Zannen desu ga, Watashi wa Shirimasen.

That's a good point, let me think about it.
それはいい指摘です。考えさせてください。
Sore wa ii shiteki desu. Kangae sasete Kudasai.

Absolutely
絶対にそうです。
Zettai ni sou Desu.

That's a possibility.
それは可能性があります。
Sore wa Kanousei ga Arimasu.

I'm open to discussion.
議論には開かれています。
Giron ni wa Hirakarete Imasu.

I'm not convinced.
私は納得していません。
Watashi wa Nattoku shite Imasen.

That's a tricky question.
それはトリッキーな質問です。
Sore wa Torikkii na Shitsumon desu.

I completely agree with you.
完全にあなたに同意します。
Kanzen ni Anata ni doui Shimasu.

I'm glad we had this conversation.
この会話をしたことをうれしく思います。
Kono kaiwa o Shita koto o ureshiku Omoimasu.

That's a possibility.
それは可能性があります。
Sore wa Kanousei ga Arimasu.

I'm open to discussion.
議論には開かれています。
Giron ni wa Hirakarete Imasu.

I'm not convinced.
私は納得していません。
Watashi wa Nattoku shite Imasen.

That's a tricky question.
それはトリッキーな質問です。
Sore wa Torikkii na Shitsumon desu.

I completely agree with you.
完全にあなたに同意します。
Kanzen ni anata ni Doui Shimasu.

I'm glad we had this conversation.
この会話をしたことをうれしく思います。
Kono kaiwa o shita Koto o ureshiku Omoimasu.

# PETS

Dog
犬
Inu

Cat
猫
Neko

Bird
鳥
Tori

Fish
魚
Sakana

Hamster
ハムスター
Hamusutā

Guinea pig
モルモット
Morumotto

Rabbit
ウサギ
Usagi

Ferret
フェレット
Feretto

Hedgehog
ハリネズミ
Harinezumi

Chinchilla
チンチラ
Chinchira

Mouse
マウス
Mausu

Rat
ネズミ
Nezumi

Gerbil
ジェルビー
Jerubī

Snake
蛇
Hebi

Lizard
トカゲ
Tokage

Tortoise
亀
Kame

Hermit crab
寄せ カニ
Yose Kani

Tarantula
タランチュラ
Taranchura

Scorpion
サソリ
Sasori

Bearded dragon
ヒゲトカゲ
Hige Tokage

Pot-bellied pig
ベトナムイノシシ
Betonamu Inoshishi

Miniature horse
ミニチュアポニー
Minichua Ponii

Goat
ヤギ
Yagi

Sheep
羊
Hitsuji

Chicken
ニワトリ
Niwa-tori

Duck
アヒル
Ahiru

How do you keep your pet healthy?
ペットの健康を保つにはどうしたらいいですか？
Pe-tto no ken-Kou wo Tamotsu ni wa Dou shitara ii Desu ka?

Do you have any tips for training a new pet?
新しいペットのしつけのヒントはありますか？
Atarashii petto no Shitsuke no hinto wa Arimasu ka?

What is your favorite thing about your pet?
ペットの好きなところは何ですか？
Pe-tto no suki na Tokoro wa nan Desu ka?

Have you ever adopted a pet from a shelter?
放棄されたペットを保護して飼ったことがありますか？
Houki sareta Petto wo Hogo shite Katta koto ga arimasu ka?

What is your pet's name?
ペットの名前は何ですか？
Pe-tto no Namae wa nan Desu ka?

Do you have any funny or heartwarming pet stories to share?
おもしろい・心温まるペットの話はありますか？
Omoshiroi / kokoro atatamaru Petto no hanashi wa Arimasu ka?

What is your opinion on spaying or neutering pets?
ペットの去勢手術や避妊手術についてどう思いますか？
Pe-tto no kyosei Shujutsu ya Hinin shujutsu ni Tsuite dou Omoimasu ka?

Have you ever had to say goodbye to a pet?
ペットとお別れしたことはありますか？
Pe-tto to o-wakare Shita koto wa Arimasu ka?

I love spending time with my pet.
ペットと過ごす時間が大好きです。
Pe-tto to Sugosu jikan ga Daisuki desu.

# COLORS

Red
赤あか
A-ka

Blue
青 or あお
A-o

Green
緑みどり
Mi-do-ri

Yellow
黄色 or きいろ
Kii-ro

Orange
オレンジ
O-ren-ji

Purple
紫 or むらさき
Mu-ra-sa-ki

Pink
ピンク
Pin-ku

Brown
茶色 or ちゃいろ
Cha-i-ro

Black
黒 or くろ
Ku-ro

White
白 or しろ
Shi-ro

Gray
灰色 or はいいろ
Hai-i-ro

Navy
濃紺 or のうこん
Nou-kon

Turquoise
空色 or そらいろ
So-ra-i-ro

Olive
オリーブ
O-ri-bu

Teal
ティール
Ti-ru

Lavende
ラベンダー
Ra-ben-daa

Beige
ベージュ
Be-jyu

Cyan
シアン
Shi-an

Salmon
サーモンピンク
Sa-mon-pinku

Gold
ゴールド
Go-ru-do

Silver
シルバー
Shi-ru-baa

Bronze
ブロンズ
Bu-ron-zu

Indigo
インディゴ
In-di-go

Fuchsia
フクシャ
Fu-ku-sha

Charcoal
チャコール
Cha-koo-ru

Peach
ピーチ
Pi-chi

Mint
ミント
Min-to

Ivory
アイボリー
Ai-bo-rii

Burgundy
バーガンディ
Ba-gan-di

Olive green
オリーブグリーン
O-ri-bu-guri-n

What's your favorite color?
あなたのお気に入りの色は何ですか？
a-na-ta no o-Ki-ni-i-ri no i-ro Wa na-ni de-su ka?

Do you like bright colors or muted ones?
鮮やかな色と落ち着いた色、どちらがお好きですか？
a-za-Ya-ka-na i-ro To o-chi-tsu-i-ta i-ro, do-chi-ra ga o-Su-ki de-su ka?

Which color do you think represents happiness?
幸せを表す色として、どの色が思い浮かびますか？
Shi-awa-se o a-ra-wa-su i-ro to-Shi-te, do-no i-ro ga
o-Mo-i-u-ka-bi-Ma-su ka?

Which color do you think represents sadness?
悲しみを表す色として、どの色が思い浮かびますか？
Ka-na-shi-mi o a-ra-wa-su i-ro to-Shi-te, do-no i-ro ga
o-Mo-i-u-ka-bi-Ma-su ka?

What color are your eyes?
私には目がないので、色はありません。
Wa-ta-shi ni wa me ga na-i no De, i-ro wa a-ri-Ma-se-n

Do you prefer warm colors or cool colors?
\温かみのある色と、涼しげな色、どちらがお好みですか？
Nu-ka-sa-mi no a-ru i-ro to, Su-zu-shi-ge-na i-ro, Do-chi-ra ga o-ko-Mi
de-su ka?

# NUMBERS

One
いち
EE-chi

Two
に
NEE

Three
さん
SAHN

Four
し or よん
SHIH or YOHN

Five
ご
GOH

Six
ろく
ROH-koo

Seven
しち or なな
SHIH-chee or NAH-nah

Eight
はち
HAH-chee

Nine
きゅう
KYOO

Ten
じゅう
JOO

Eleven
じゅういち
JOO-EE-chi

Twelve
じゅうに
JOO-NEE

Thirteen
じゅうさん
JOO-SAHN

Fourteen
じゅうし or じゅうよん
JOO-SHIH or JOO-YOHN

Fifteen
じゅうご
JOO-GOH

Sixteen
じゅうろく
JOO-ROH-koo

Seventeen
じゅうしち or じゅうなな
JOO-SHIH-chee or JOO-NAH-nah

Eighteen
じゅうはち
JOO-HAH-chee

Nineteen
じゅうきゅう
JOO-KYOO

Twenty
にじゅう
NEE-joo

# HANDLING A RUDE PERSON

Please don't speak to me like that
そんな言い方をしないでください。
Son-na ii-kata o Shi-na-i-de ku-Da-sai

Let's keep this conversation respectful
この会話は敬意をもって行いましょう。
Ko-no kai-wa wa kei-i o Mot-te i-na-i-de Ku-da-sai

I don't appreciate the tone you're using
あなたの言い方には不快感を覚えます。
A-na-ta no ii-kata ni wa Fu-kai-kan o o-Bo-e-ma-Su

That's not an appropriate way to communicate
そんな話し方は適切ではありません。
Son-na ha-na-Shi-kata wa Tekki-setsu de wa a-ri-Ma-sen

Let's try to stay calm and find a solution
落ち着いて解決策を見つけましょう。
O-chi-tsui-te ka-i-Ketsu-saku o mi-Tsu-ke-ma-Sho-u

I'm sorry, but I won't tolerate that kind of behavior
ごめんなさい、そのような行動は許容できません。
Go-men-na-sai, son-na Yo-u-na ko-u-do wa Kyo-yo- de-ki-Ma-se-n

I don't appreciate the way you're speaking to me
あなたの話し方には不快感を覚えます。
A-na-ta no ha-na-shi-Kata ni wa fu-kai-Kan o o-bo-e-Ma-su

I understand you're upset, but please don't take it out on me
あなたが怒っているのは分かりますが、私に八つ当たりしない
でください。
A-na-ta ga okot-te i-ru no wa wa-Ka-ri-ma-su ga, wa-Ta-shi ni
ya-tsu-a-Ta-ri shi-na-i-De ku-da-sai

Let's try to stay calm and talk this through
落ち着いて話し合いましょう。
O-chi-Tsui-te ha-na-Shi-ai-ma-Sho-u

Can we please have a civil conversation?
礼儀正しい会話をしましょうか？
Re-i-gi-ta-da-shii Kai-wa o shi-Ma-sho-u Ka?

Please watch your language when you're talking to me
私に話しかけるときは言葉遣いに気をつけてください。
Wa-ta-shi ni ha-na-Shi-ka-ke-ru to-Ki wa ko-to-ba-Tsu-ka-i ni ki-o
Tsu-ke-te ku-Da-Sai

I don't deserve to be spoken to in that way
そんな言い方をされるのは当然ではありません。
Son-na ii-kata o sa-reru no wa To-u-zen de Wa a-ri-ma-Se-n

Your behavior is unacceptable.
あなたのふるまいは受け入れられません。
Anata no Furumai wa ukeire Raremasen.

I'm not going to engage in this kind of disrespect.
このような不遜な態度には応じません。
Kono yōna Fusonna taido ni wa Ojimasen.

I won't be spoken to like that.
そんな風に話しかけられたくありません。
Sonna kaze ni Hanashikakeraretaku Arimasen.

I won't tolerate rude or aggressive behavior.
失礼で攻撃的な態度は許しません。
Shitsurei de Kōgekiteki na taido wa Yurushimasen.

Please treat me with respect.
尊重して扱ってください。
Sonchō shite atsukatte kudasai.

I don't think it's appropriate to speak to anyone in that manner.
そのようなやり方で誰にでも話しかけるべきではないと思います。
Sono yōna Yarikata de Dare ni demo hanashikakeru Beki de wa nai to Omoimasu.

I won't engage in an argument with you.
あなたと論争に巻き込まれたくありません。
Anata to ronsō ni Makikomaretaku Arimasen.

I'd appreciate it if you would speak to me more respectfully.
もっと尊重して話しかけていただけるとありがたいです。
Motto Sonchō shite Hanashikakete itadakeru to arigatai Desu.

Please lower your voice.
声を落としてください。
Koe wo otoshite Kudasai

Your behavior is making me uncomfortable.
あなたの行動は私を不快にさせています。
Anata no kōdō wa Watashi wo fukai ni Saseteimasu.

I won't put up with this kind of treatment.
このような扱いには耐えられません。
Kono yōna atsukai ni wa Taeraremasen

Please show some respect.
尊重を示してください。
Sonchō Wo Hyōji Shite Kudasai.

I won't stand for this.
このような扱いを受け入れません。
Kono yōna Atsukai o Ukeiremasen

Please stop speaking to me in that manner.
その言い方をやめてください。
Sono Iikata o Yamete Kudasai

I'm not going to listen to this kind of language.
このような言葉は聞きたくありません。
Kono yōna Kotoba wa kikitaku Arimasen

I won't tolerate this disrespectful behavior
このような失礼な態度は許しません。
Kono yōna Shitsurei na Taido wa Yurushimasen

Please calm down and let's talk rationally.
落ち着いて冷静に話しましょう。
Ochitsuite reisei ni Hanashimashou

I don't appreciate being spoken to like that.
そのような言い方をされるのは好ましくありません。
Sono yōna iikata o Sareru no wa Konomashikuarimase.

Please refrain from using offensive language.
不快な言葉遣いは控えてください。
Fukai na Kotobazukai wa Hikaete Kudasai

Please don't speak to me like that.
そのように話しかけないでください
Sono yōni Hanashikakenaide Kudasai

Let's keep this conversation respectful.
この会話を敬意をもって続けましょう。
Kono kaiwa o Keii o motte Tsudzukemashou.

I don't appreciate the tone you're using.
その口調は好ましくありません。
Sono Kuchō wa Konomashikuarimasen

That's not an appropriate way to communicate.
それは適切なコミュニケーションの方法ではありません。
Sore wa Tekisetsuna komyunikeeshon no Hōhō de wa Arimasen

Let's try to stay calm and find a solution.
落ち着いて解決策を見つけましょう。
Ochitsuite Kaiketsusaku o Mitsukemashou

# AT THE DENTIST

I have an appointment with Dr. _____.
____先生の予約をしています。
Sensei-no-Yoyaku-o-Shiteimasu

I'm here for my dental checkup.
歯科検診に来ました。
Shika-kenshin-ni-Kimashita

I need to schedule a cleaning.
クリーニングの予約をしたいのですが。
Kuri-ningu-no-Yoyaku-o-shitai-no-Desu-Ga

I have a toothache.
歯が痛いです。
Ha-ga-Itai-Desu

I'm experiencing sensitivity in my teeth.
歯がしみる感じがあります。
Ha-ga-Shimiru-kanji-ga-Arimasu

I broke a tooth and need it repaired.
歯が折れたので修復してほしいです。
Ha-Ga-oreta-node-Shu-fuku-Shite-hoshii-Desu

I lost a filling and need it replaced.
詰め物が取れたので修復してほしいです。
tsumemono-ga-toreta-node-shu-fuku-shite-hoshii-desu

I have a cavity that needs to be filled.
虫歯があるので、詰め物をしてほしいです。
Mushiba-Ga-aru-Node-Tsumemono-o-Shite-hoshii-Desu

I need a dental X-ray.
レントゲンを撮りたいのですが。
Rentogen-o-Tori-tai-no-Desu-ga

I'm interested in teeth whitening.
歯のホワイトニングに興味があります。
ha-No-howaito-Ningu-ni-kyo-mi-ga-Arimasu

Can you recommend a good toothpaste?
いい歯磨き粉をおすすめしていただけますか？
ii Hamigaki ko wo Osusume Shite itadakemasu ka?

How often should I floss?
どのくらいの頻度でフロスを使うべきですか？
Donokurai no Hindo de furosu wo Tsukau beki Desu ka?

Do you have any tips for improving my dental hygiene?
歯の健康を改善するためのアドバイスをいただけますか？
ha no Kenkou wo kaizen Suru tame no Adobaisu wo Itadakemasu ka?

How long will the procedure take?
治療にはどのくらい時間がかかりますか？
Chiryou ni wa Donokurai jikan ga Kakarimasu ka?

Will I need any anesthesia?
麻酔は必要ですか？
Masui wa Hitsuyou Desu ka?

How much will the procedure cost?
治療にはどのくらい費用がかかりますか？
Chiryou ni wa Donokurai hiyou ga Kakarimasu ka?

Do you accept insurance?
保険は使えますか？
HOKEN wa Tsukaemasu ka?

Can you explain the procedure to me?
手順を教えていただけますか？
TEJUN wo oshiete itadakemasu ka?

Is there any discomfort associated with the procedure?
手順に不快な感覚はありますか？
TEJUN ni fukai na kankaku wa arimasu ka?

How long will it take for me to recover?
回復にどのくらいの時間がかかりますか？
KAIFUKU ni dono kurai no jikan ga kakarimasu ka?

Can I eat or drink anything before the procedure?
手順の前に何か食べたり飲んだりしてもいいですか？
TEJUN no mae ni nanika tabetari nondari shitemo ii desu ka?

Will I need someone to drive me home after the procedure?
処置後に運転をする人が必要ですか
Shochi-go ni Unten o suru hito Ga hitsuyou Desu ka?

Will I need to take any medication after the procedure?
手術後、薬を服用する必要がありますか？
Shujutsu-go, KUSURI wo fukuyou suru hitsuyou ga arimasu ka?

Can you give me a prescription for pain medication?
痛み止めの処方箋を出してもらえますか？
Itami-dome no Shohousen wo Dashite moraemasu ka?

How often should I come in for a checkup?
検診はどのくらいの頻度で受けるべきですか？
Kenshin wa Dono kurai No hindo de Ukeru beki desu ka?

Can you recommend any oral hygiene products
口腔衛生用品をおすすめしてもらえますか？
Koukou Eisei youhin wo Osusume shite Moraemasu ka?

Can you show me how to properly brush and floss my teeth?
正しい歯磨きやフロスの使い方を教えてもらえますか？
Tadashii hamigaki ya FUROSU no tsukaikata wo oshiete Moraemasu ka?

Do you have any aftercare instructions for me?
アフターケアの指示はありますか？
Afutaakea no Shiji wa Arimasu ka?

Can you schedule my next appointment?
次回の予約をしていただけますか？
Jikai no yoyaku wo Shite itadakemasu ka?

Thank you, see you next time.
ありがとうございます、また次回。
Arigatou gozaimasu, Mata jikai.

# COMMON QUESTIONS IN A NEW COUNTRY

Where is the nearest bank or ATM?
最寄りの銀行やATMはどこですか？
Moyori no ginkou ya ATM wa doko desu ka?

What is the country's official language?
国の公用語は何ですか？
Kuni no Kouyougo wa Nan Desu ka?

How do I get to my accommodation?
宿泊先にはどうやって行けばいいですか？
Shukuhaku saki ni wa Dou yatte ikeba ii Desu ka?

What is the local transportation system like?
地元の交通システムはどんな感じですか？
Jimoto no Koutsu Shisutemu wa Donna kanji Desu ka?

Are there any cultural customs or practices that I should be aware of?
注意すべき文化的な慣習はありますか？
Chuui subeki Bunkateki na kanshou wa Arimasu ka?

What are the local emergency numbers?
現地の緊急電話番号は何ですか？
Genchi no Kinkyuu Denwa bangou wa Nan desu ka?

Is there a tourist information center nearby?
近くに観光案内所はありますか？
Chikaku ni kankou Annaijo wa Arimasu ka?

Are there any local festivals or events happening soon?
近々地元のお祭りやイベントはありますか？
Chikajiku jimoto no Omatsuri ya ibento wa Arimasu ka?

Where are the best places to eat or drink?
食事や飲み物をするのに最適な場所はどこですか？
Shokuji ya Nomimono wo Suru no ni saiteki na Basho wa doko Desu ka?

What are the must-see tourist attractions?
必見の観光スポットは何ですか？
Hikken No kankou Supotto wa Nan Desu ka?

How do I say common phrases in the local language?
地元の言葉でよく使われるフレーズはどうやって言いますか？
Jimoto No kotoba de yoku Tsukawareru Fureezu wa dou yatte ii Masu ka?

How much does public transportation cost?
公共交通機関はどのくらいの値段ですか？
Koukyou Koutsu kikan wa Dono kurai no Nedan Desu ka?

Can you recommend a good restaurant nearby?
近くのおすすめのレストランを教えていただけますか？
Chikaku No Osusume no Resutoran wo oshiete itadakemasu ka?

Can you recommend a good place to shop?
良いお店を教えていただけますか？
yo-i o-Mi-se wo o-Shie-Te i-ta-da-ke-Mas ka?

Is it safe to walk around the area at night?
夜にその地域を歩くのは安全ですか？
yo-Ru ni so-No chi-Iki wo a-Ru-ku no Wa an-zen Des ka?

Where can I find a good pharmacy?
良い薬局はどこにありますか？
yo-i ya-ku-Kyo ku Wa Do-ko ni a-ri-Mas ka?

Can you recommend a good place to stay?
良い宿泊先を教えていただけますか？
yo-i Shu-ku-ha-ku-Sa-ki wo o-Shie-te i-ta-Da-ke-mas ka?

What is the weather like at this time of year?

この時期の天気はどうですか？

No-No ji-ki no Ten-ki wa Dou des ka?


What is the local time?

現地の時間は何時ですか？

Gen-Chi No ji-kan wa Nan-ji Des ka?


How do I get a local phone number?

地元の電話番号はどうやって手に入れますか？

Chi-mo-To No den-Wa ban-go wa Dou-ya-tte te Ni i-re-Mas ka?


What are the emergency numbers in this country?

この国の緊急電話番号は何ですか？

ko-no kuni no kin-kyuu den-wa ban-go wa nan des ka?


Can you recommend a good local guide or tour company?

良い地元のガイドやツアー会社をお勧めいただけますか？

yo-i Chi-mo-to no Ga-i-Do ya Tsu-a-ka-i-sha wo O-su-se-me
i-ta-Da-ke-mas ka?


How do I get from the airport to my accommodation?

空港から宿泊先までの行き方を教えてください

Kuu-kou Ka-ra shu-Ku-ha-ku-Sa-ki Ma-de no i-ki-Ka-Ta wo o-Shie-te
ku-Da-sai?

# POLITE RESPONSES

Thank you
ありがとうございます
Ah-ree-gah-toh Goh-zai-Mahs

Excuse me, please
すみません、お願いします
Su-mi-Mah-sen, oh-nah-Gah-ee-Shee-Mahs

I'm sorry
ごめんなさい
Go-Men-Nah-Sigh

Please
お願いします
Oh-Gah-gah-Ee-Shee-Mahs

May I help you?
お手伝いしましょうか？
Oh-teh-tsu-Dah-yee Shee-mah-Mhoh-ka?

Nice to meet you
初めまして
Ha-Jee-meh-Mah-sh-teh

After you
お先にどうぞ
Oh-sah-Keh-nee-Dohh-Zoh

Pardon me
すみません
Su-mi-Mah-Sen

Thank you for your help
助けてくれてありがとう
Tas-keh-teh Koo-reh-Teh Ah-ree-Gah-toh

May I?
してもよろしいですか？
She-teh Moh yoh-roh-Shee-ee Des-ka?

Could you?
していただけませんか？
She-Teh ee-tah-Dah-keh-Mah-sen-ka?

Would you mind?
構いませんか？
Koh-mah-ee-Mah-Sehn-ka?

I'm sorry
ごめんなさい
Go-meh-Nah-Sigh

Go ahead
どうぞ
Doh-Zoh

No problem
問題ありません
Mon-Dai a-ri-Ma-sen

It was my pleasure
どういたしまして
Doh-Ee-tah-Shee-mah-Shee-the

My apologies
お詫び申し上げます
Oh-wa-Bi mo-Shi-a-ge-Ma-su

With all due respect
失礼ありますが
Shi-tsu-Rei a-ri-Ma-su-Ga

95

If you don't mind
よろしければ
Yo-ro-Shi-ke-Re-B

If it's not too much trouble
お手数でなければ
O-te-suu-De na-ke-Re-Ba

Thank you kindly
どうもありがとうございます
Doh-mo a-ri-Ga-toh go-Za-i-ma-Su

You're welcome
どういたしまして
Doh-ee-tah-Shee-Mah-Shee-the

No, thank you
いいえ、けっこうです
Ee-eh, Kek-koh Desu

If I may ask
お尋ねしてもよろしいでしょうか
O-ta-na-e Shi-te Mo yo-ro-shi-i De-Sho-u ka

Thank you for your time
時間を割いていただきありがとうございます。
Jikan Wo Saite itadaki Arigatou Gozaimasu

It's been a pleasure
楽しかったです。
Tanoshikatta Desu

I appreciate it
感謝しています。
Kansha Shiteimasu

I'll be happy to help
お手伝いできて嬉しいです。
O-Tetsudai Dekite Ureshii Desu

That's very kind of you
とても親切なことをしていただきました。
Totemo Shinsetsu Na koto Wo shite Itadakimashita

Thank you in advance
お先にありがとうございます。
O-saki ni Arigatou Gozaimasu

Excuse me for interrupting
ごめんください
Mo-Men ku-da-Sai

I appreciate your help
ご協力ありがとうございます
Go-kyo-Ryoku a-ri-ga-To-u go-Za-i-Ma-su

Please let me know
お知らせください
O-shi-ra-Se ku-Da-Sai

May I ask a question?
質問してもよろしいでしょうか
Shi-tsu-mon Shi-te Mo yo-ro-shi-i De-sho-u ka

Could you repeat that, please?
もう一度言っていただけますか
mo-u i-Chi-do it-tte i-ta-Da-ke-ma-su ka

Would you be so kind as to...
お願いできませんか
O-ne-gai De-ki-ma-Se-n ka

I'm sorry to bother you
お手数おかけしてすみません
O-te-su-To-o-ka-ke-Shi-te Su-mi-Ma-se-n

After you, please
どうぞお先に
Do-u-zo o-Sa-ki-Ni

Thank you for your understanding
ご理解いただきありがとうございます
Go-ri-kai i-ta-da-ki A-ri-ga-to-u Go-za-i-Ma-su

No, thank you, I'm good
いいえ、結構です
I-i-E, kek-Ko-u De-su

Please, take a seat
お座りください
O-su-Wa-ri ku-Da-sai

I'll do my best
がんばります
Gan-Ba-ri-ma-Su

Thank you for your patience
お待ちいただきありがとうございます
O-Ma-chi i-Ta-da-ki A-ri-ga-to-u Go-za-i-Ma-su

May I offer you something to drink?
何か飲み物をご用意しましょうか
Na-ni-Ka no-mi-Mo-No o go-yo-u-i Shi-ma-sho-u ka

Would you like me to help you?
手伝いましょうか
Te-tsu-Da-i ma-Sho-u ka

I beg your pardon
ごめんください
Go-Men ku-Da-sai

I didn't catch that
聞き取れませんでした
Ki-ki-to-Re-ma-se-N-De-Shi-ta

If it's not too much trouble
もしよろしければ
Mo-shi-yo-ro-Shi-ke-Re-ba

Thank you for your hospitality
おもてなしいただきありがとうございます
O-mo-te-Na-shi-i-Ta-da-ki a-ri-Ga-to-u Go-za-i-ma-su

That's very generous of you
ご厚意に感謝します
Go-kou-i ni Kan-sha Shi-Ma-su

Please accept my apologies
申し訳ありません
Mo-shi-wa-Ke a-ri-Ma-se-n

If I may make a suggestion...
提案があれば
Tei-an Ga a-re-Ba

I'm sorry, I didn't mean to
ごめんなさい、そうするつもりではなかったです
Go-men-na-sai, sou su-ru tsu-mo-ri de-wa-na-ka-tta de-su

Thank you for taking the time
お時間いただきありがとうございます
O-ji-kan i-Ta-Da-ki a-ri-Ga-to-u go-Za-i-ma-su

May I offer you a hand?
手伝って差し上げましょうか？
Te-tsu-da-Tte Sa-shi-a-Ge-ma-Shou-ka?

My apologies for the inconvenience
ご迷惑をおかけしました
Go-mei-wa-ku O o-ka-Ke shi-Ma-shi-ta

Please forgive me
お許しください
O-yu-ru-Shi-ku-Da-sai

Thank you for your time and attention
お時間とご配慮いただきありがとうございます
O-ji-kan To go-hai-Ryo i-ta-Da-ki a-ri-Ga-to-u go-Za-i-ma-su

It was nice meeting you
お会いできてよかったです
O-ai-de-ki-te Yo-ka-Tta de-su

Excuse me, would you happen to know...?
すみません、ご存知ですか？
Su-mi-ma-Sen, Go-zon-ji De-su ka?

# DESCRIBING PEOPLE

She's kind and helpful.
彼女は親切で助けたい気持ちがある。
Ka-no-jo Wa shin-Setsu de Tasu-ke-Tai ki-mo-chi Ga a-ru

He's smart and hardworking.
彼は賢くて働き者です。
Ka-re Wa ka-Shi-ka-te Hat-ta-ri De-su

She's creative and talented.
彼女は創造力に富み、才能がある。
Ka-no-jo wa Sou-zou-Ryoku ni to-Mi, Sai-nou Ga a-Ru

He's confident and charismatic.
彼は自信にあふれ、カリスマ性がある。
Ka-re Wa ji-Shin ni a-Fu-re, ka-ri-Su-sei Ga a-ru

She's reliable and responsible.
彼女は信頼でき、責任感がある。
Ka-no-jo wa Shin-rai De-ki, se-ki-Nin-kan Ga a-ru

Confident
自信がある
ji-Shin Ga a-Ru

Cautious
用心深い
you-Shin Bu-ka-i

Brave
勇敢な
yu-u-Kan-Na

Fearful
恐れ多い
O-so-Re-o-O-i

Careless
不注意な
Fu-Chuu-i-Na

Meticulous
細心な
Sai-Shin-Na

Energetic
エネルギッシュな
E-ne-Ru-gi-Shu-na

Laid-back
のんびりした
Non-bi-Ri-shi-Ta

Creative
クリエイティブな
Ku-ri-E-i-ti-Bu-na

Logical
論理的な
Ron-Ri-te-ki-Na

Ambitious
野心的な
ya-Shin-Te-ki-Na

Humble
謙虚な
Ken-Kyo-Na

Arrogant
傲慢な
Go-Man-Na

Thoughtful
思慮深い
Shi-Ryo Bu-ka-i

Impulsive
衝動的な
Shou-Dou-te-Ki-na

Patient
忍耐強い
Nin-tai Tsu-yoi

Impatient
気が短い
Ki Ga mi-ji-Kai

Sociable
社交的な
Sha-Kou-Te-ki-Na

Reserved
控えめな
Hi-ka-E-Me-na

Reliable
信頼できる
Shin-Rai de-Ki-ru

Unreliable
信頼できない
Shin-rai De-ki-Na-i

Diligent
勤勉な
Kin-Ben-Na

Lazy
怠惰な
Tai-da-na

Outgoing
外向的な
Gai-Kou-Te-ki-na

Introverted
内向的な
Nai-kou-Te-ki-Na

Impressive
印象的な
In-shou-Te-ki-Na

Mediocre
平凡な
Hei-Bon-Na

Enthusiastic
熱心な
Ne-Sshin-Na

Lackadaisical
だらしのない
Da-ra-Shi-no-Na-i

Punctual
時間に正確な
ji-kan ni Se-i-Kaku-Na

# DESCRIBING THINGS

The view is beautiful
眺めが美しい
Nagame Ga Utsukushii

The decor is stylish
装飾がおしゃれ
Sōshoku Ga Oshare

The food is delicious
食べ物がおいしい
Tabemono Ga Oishii

The room is cozy
部屋が居心地がいい
Heya Ga igokochi Ga ii

The car is luxurious
車が高級
Kuruma Ga Kōkyū

# MAKING A SUGGESTION

Let's try something new
あたらしいことをしてみましょう
A-ta-ra-shi-i ko-to wo Shi-te mi-Ma-sho-u

How about we do this...
これをやってみましょう
Ko-re wo ya-tte mi-ma-sho-u

Maybe we could
たぶん、私たちはできるかもしれません
Ta-Bun, wa-Ta-shi-ta-Chi Wa de-ki-Ru ka-mo-Shi-re-ma-su

Why don't we consider...
を考慮してみませんか
Wo ko-u-ryo Shi-te mi-Ma-se-n ka

What if we try...
もし試してみたらどうですか
Mo-shi, shi-te Mi-ta-ra dou De-su ka

I suggest.
私は提案します
Wa-ta-shi wa Te-i-an Shi-ma-su

Perhaps we could
ひょっとしたら私たちはできるかもしれません
Hyo-tto shi-ta-ra Wa-ta-shi-ta-Chi wa de-ki-ru Ka-mo-Shi-re-ma-su

How about we explore...
探検してみましょう
Tan-ken Shi-te mi-Ma-sho-u

106

Why don't we brainstorm?
アイデアを出し合ってみませんか
Ai-de-a wo Da-shi-a-tte Mi-ma-se-N ka

How about we...
〜はどうでしょう
Wa dou De-sho-u

Why don't we...
〜しませんか
Shi-ma-Se-n Ka

Have you considered...
考えたことがありますか
kan-Gae-ta ko-to Ga a-ri-Ma-su ka

Would you like to...
〜しませんか
Shi-ma-Se-n ka

# HOBBIES AND INTERESTS

What do you like to do in your free time?
あなたは暇な時間に何をしたいですか？
Anata wa hima Na jikan ni Nani O shitai desu ka?

Do you play any sports or have any favorite teams
スポーツをしていますか？好きなチームはありますか？
Supotsu o Shite imasu ka?

What kind of books do you like to read?
どのような本を読むのが好きですか？
Dono youna Hon o yomu no Ga suki desu ka?

Do you enjoy cooking as well?
あなたは料理をするのが好きですか？
Anata wa ryouri o Suru no Ga suki Desu ka?

Have you traveled to any interesting places lately?
最近、面白い場所に旅行しましたか？
Saikin, Omoshiroi Basho ni ryokou Shimashita ka?

What kind of music do you like?
どんな音楽が好きですか？
Donna ongaku Ga suki Desu ka?

Do you enjoy spending time in nature?
自然の中で時間を過ごすのが好きですか？
Shizen no Naka de jikan o Sugosu no Ga suki Desu ka?

Do you have any favorite artists or types of art?
お気に入りのアーティストやアートの種類はありますか？
Okiniiri no Aatisto ya Aato no Shurui wa Arimasu ka?

What kind of hobbies do you enjoy doing at home?
家で楽しむ趣味は何ですか？
Le de Tanoshimu Shumi wa Nan Desu ka?


My favorite hobby is reading books.
私の趣味は本を読むことです。
Watashi no Shumi wa Hon o yomu Koto Desu.


I like to go for long walks in nature.
私は自然の中を長い散歩することが好きです。
Watashi wa Shizen no Naka o nagai Sanpo suru Koto ga suki Desu.


I enjoy watching movies and TV shows.
私は映画やテレビ番組を観ることが楽しいです。
Watashi Wa eiga ya Terebi Bangumi O miru koto ga Tanoshii Desu.


My favorite hobby is photography.
私の趣味は写真を撮ることです。
Watashi no Shumi wa Shashin o Toru koto desu.


I love listening to music and attending concerts.
私は音楽を聴くこととコンサートに行くことが大好きです。
Watashi wa Ongaku o kiku Koto to konsaato ni iku Koto ga Daisuki
desu.


I enjoy cooking and trying new recipes.
私は料理をすることと新しいレシピを試すことが楽しいです。
Watashi wa ryouri o Suru koto to Atarashii Reshipi o Tamesu koto Ga
tanoshii Desu.


I like to travel and explore new places
私は旅行して新しい場所を探検することが好きです。
Watashi wa Ryokou shite Atarashii Basho o tanken Buru koto Ga suki
desu.


My favorite hobby is painting and drawing
私の趣味は絵を描くことです。
Watashi no Shumi wa e o Kaku koto Desu.

I enjoy gardening and growing my own vegetables.
私はガーデニングと自分で野菜を育てることが楽しいです。
Watashi wa Gaadeningu to Jibun de yasai O sodateru koto Ga tanoshii Desu.

I like to do DIY projects around the house.
私は家の周りでDIYプロジェクトをすることが好きです。
Watashi wa ie no mawari De DIY purojekuto o Suru koto ga Suki desu.

My favorite hobby is playing sports, especially soccer.
私の趣味はスポーツをすることで、特にサッカーが好きです。
Watashi no Shumi wa supootsu o Suru koto de, Tokuni sakkā Ga suki Desu.

I love to dance and take dance classes.
私は踊ることが大好きで、ダンスクラスを受けるのも好きす。
Watashi wa Odoru koto Ga daisuki de, Dansu kurasu o Ukeru no mo suki Desu.

I enjoy playing video games.
私はビデオゲームをするのが好きです。
Watashi wa Bideo geemu O suru no Ga suki desu.

My favorite hobby is reading books.
私の趣味は本を読むことです。
Watashi No shumi Wa hon o yomu koto Desu.

I like to go for long walks in nature.
私は自然の中を長い散歩することが好きです。
Watashi wa shizen No naka o Nagai sanpo Suru koto Ga suki Desu.

I enjoy watching movies and TV shows.
私は映画やテレビ番組を観ることが楽しいです。
Watashi wa Eiga ya terebi Bangumi o Miru koto ga Tanoshii Desu.

My favorite hobby is photography.
私の趣味は写真を撮ることです。
Watashi no shumi wa shashin o toru koto desu.

I love listening to music and attending concerts.

私は音楽を聴くこととコンサートに行くことが大好きです。

Watashi wa ongaku o kiku koto to konsaato ni iku koto ga daisuki desu.

I enjoy cooking and trying new recipes.

私は料理をすることと新しいレシピを試すことが楽しいです。

Watashi wa Ryouri o suru Koto to atarashii Reshipi o tamesu koto Ga tanoshii Desu.

I like to travel and explore new places.

私は旅行して新しい場所を探検することが好きです。

Watashi wa Ryokou Shite atarashii Basho o Tanken Suru koto ga suki Desu.

My favorite hobby is painting and drawing.

私の趣味は絵を描くことです。

Watashi no Shumi wa e o Kaku koto Desu

I enjoy gardening and growing my own vegetables.

私はガーデニングと自分で野菜を育てることが楽しいです。

Watashi wa Gaadeningu to Jibun de yasai o sodateru koto Ga tanoshii Desu.

I like to do DIY projects around the house

私は家の周りでDIYプロジェクトをすることが好きです。

Watashi wa ie no Mawari de DIY purojekuto o Suru koto ga suki Desu.

My favorite hobby is playing sports, especially soccer.

私の趣味はスポーツをすることで、特にサッカーが好きです。

Watashi no shumi wa Supootsu o Suru koto de, Tokuni sakkā ga suki Desu.

I love to dance and take dance classes.

私は踊ることが大好きで、ダンスクラスを受けるのも好きです。

Watashi wa Odoru koto ga Daisuki de, dansu Kurasu o ukeru No mo suki Desu

I enjoy writing and journaling.
私は書くことと日記をつけることが楽しいです。
Watashi wa Kaku koto to Nikki o tsukeru koto ga Tanoshii desu.

My favorite hobby is watching and analyzing sports games.
私の好きな趣味はスポーツの試合を観戦して分析することです。
Watashi no sukina Shumi wa SUPOTSU no shiai wo kansen shite Bunseki suru koto Desu.

I like to collect stamps and coins
切手やコインを収集するのが好きです。
Kitte ya KOIN wo Shuushuu Suru no ga suki Desu.

I enjoy going to the gym and working out.
ジムでトレーニングするのが楽しいです。
JIMU de TOREENINGU suru no Ga tanoshii Desu.

I like to go fishing and camping.
釣りやキャンプに行くのが好きです。
Tsuri ya KYANPU ni iku no Ga suki Desu.

My favorite hobby is playing board games with friends.
私の好きな趣味は友達とボードゲームをすることです。
Watashi no sukina shumi wa tomodachi to BOODO GEEMU wo suru koto desu.

I love to go to the theater and see live performances.
劇場に行ってライブパフォーマンスを見ることが大好きです。
Gekijou ni itte RAIBU PAFOOMANSU wo miru koto ga daisuki desu.

I enjoy attending art exhibitions and museums.
美術展や博物館に行くのが楽しいです。
Bijutsu ten ya Hakubutsukan ni iku no ga tanoshii Desu.

My favorite hobby is practicing yoga and meditation.
私の好きな趣味はヨガや瞑想をすることです。
Watashi no sukina Shumi wa YOGA ya meiso wo Suru koto desu.

I like to do crossword puzzles and other brain teasers.
クロスワードパズルや他の頭脳トレーニングが好きです。
KUROSUWAADO PAZURU ya hoka no zunou TOREENINGU ga suki
desu.

I love to read and write poetry.
詩を読んだり書いたりするのが大好きです。
Shi wo yondari kaitari Suru no Ga daisuki Desu.

My favorite hobby is woodworking and carpentry.
私の好きな趣味は木工や大工仕事です。
Watashi no Sukina shumi Wa mokkou ya Daiku shigoto Desu.

I like to go to the beach and spend time by the water.
海辺で時間を過ごすのが好きです。
Umibe de jikan wo sugosu no ga suki desu.

I enjoy playing chess and other strategy games.
チェスや他の戦略ゲームをするのが楽しいです。
Chesu ya hoka No senryaku Ge-mu wo suru No ga tanoshii Desu

My favorite hobby is birdwatching and observing wildlife.
鳥見や野生動物の観察がお気に入りの趣味です。
Torimi ya yasei Dobutsu No Kansatsu ga Okiniiri no Shumi desu

I enjoy attending festivals and cultural events.
祭りや文化イベントに参加するのが楽しいです。
Matsuri ya Bunka ibento Ni sanka Suru no Ga tanoshii Desu

I love to go to amusement parks and ride roller coasters.
遊園地に行ってジェットコースターに乗るのが大好きです。
yuuenchi Ni itte Jetto ko-suta- Ni noru no ga Daisuki desu

My favorite hobby is collecting vinyl records.
ビニールレコードを収集することが私のお気に入りの趣味です。
Bin-ru Rek-do wo Shuushuu Suru Koto ga Watashi No okiniiri no Shumi
desu

I like to go on long road trips and explore new places.
長距離のドライブをして新しい場所を探検するのが好きです。
Choukyori no Doraibu wo shite Atarashii basho Wo tanken suru No ga suki Desu

I enjoy hiking and camping in the mountains.
山登りやキャンプが好きです。
yamagari ya Kyanpu ga Suki Desu

My favorite hobby is baking and trying new dessert recipes.
お菓子作りと新しいレシピを試すことが私のお気に入りの趣味です。
Okashi tsukuri to Atarashii reshipi wo Tamesu koto ga Watashi no okiniiri No shumi Desu

I like to practice meditation and mindfulness.
瞑想やマインドフルネスを実践するのが好きです。
Meisou ya Maindofurunesu wo jissen Suru no ga suki Desu

I love to go to the zoo and see all the animals.
動物園に行ってすべての動物を見るのが大好きです。
Doubutsuen ni Itte Subete no Doubutsu wo Miru no ga daisuki Desu

My favorite hobby is studying different languages.
異なる言語を勉強することが私のお気に入りの趣味です。
Kotonaru Gengo wo Benkyou suru koto Ga watashi no Okiniiri no shumi Desu

I enjoy watching documentaries and learning new things.
ドキュメンタリーを見て新しいことを学ぶのが楽しいです。
Dokyumentari- wo Mite atarashii koto wo Manabu no ga tanoshii Desu

I like to practice yoga and pilates for exercise.
私はエクササイズのためにヨガやピラティスをするのが好きです。
Watashi wa EKU-SA-I-ZU no tame ni YO-GA ya PI-RA-TI-SU wo suru no ga suki desu.

I enjoy going to concerts and listening to live music.
私はコンサートに行ってライブ音楽を聴くのが楽しいです。
Watashi wa KON-SA-TO ni itte RA-I-BU O-NGA-KU wo kiku no ga
TANOshi desu.

My favorite hobby is doing puzzles and brain teasers.
私の趣味はパズルや脳トレをすることです。
Watashi no SHU-MI wa PA-ZU-RU ya NOU-TO-RE wo suru koto desu.

I like to go on bike rides and explore new trails.
私は自転車に乗って新しい道を探索するのが好きです。
Watashi wa JITEN-SHA ni notte ATARASHII MICHI wo TANsaku suru no
ga suki desu.

I love to read and watch sci-fi and fantasy movies.
私はSFやファンタジーの映画を読んだり見たりするのが大好き
です。
Watashi wa SF ya FAN-TA-JI- no eiga wo yon dari mi tari suru no ga
DAIsuki desu.

My favorite hobby is playing video games with friends.
私の趣味は友達とビデオゲームをすることです。
Watashi no SHU-MI wa TOMO-DACHI to BI-DE-O GE-MU wo suru koto
desu.

I like to go to the park and have picnics with my family.
私は家族と公園でピクニックをするのが好きです
Watashi wa KAZOKU to KOU-EN de PI-KU-NIK-KU wo suru no ga suki
desu.

My favorite hobby is watching and analyzing sports games.
私の趣味はスポーツの試合を観戦して分析することです。
Watashi no Shumi wa Supootsu no Shiai wo kansen Shite bunseki suru
koto Desu.

I like to collect stamps and coins.
私は切手やコインを集めることが好きです。
Watashi wa Kitte ya koin wo Atsumeru koto ga suki Desu.

I enjoy going to the gym and working out.
ジムに行って運動するのが楽しいです。
Jimu ni itte Undou suru no Ga tanoshii Desu.

I like to go fishing and camping.
釣りやキャンプに行くのが好きです。
Tsurii ya kyanpu ni iku No ga suki Desu.

My favorite hobby is playing board games with friends.
私の趣味は友達とボードゲームをすることです。
Watashi no shumi Wa tomodachi to Boodo Geemu wo Suru koto Desu.

I love to go to the theater and see live performances.
劇場に行ってライブパフォーマンスを見るのが大好きです。
Gekijou ni itte raibu pafoumansu Wo Miru no ga daisuki Desu.

I enjoy attending art exhibitions and museums.
美術展や博物館に行くのが楽しいです。
Bijutsuten ya Hakubutsukan Ni iku no ga Tanoshii Desu.

My favorite hobby is practicing yoga and meditation.
私の趣味はヨガや瞑想をすることです。
Watashi no shumi wa yoga ya meisou wo suru koto desu.

I like to do crossword puzzles and other brain teasers.
クロスワードパズルや他の頭脳トレーニングが好きです。
Kurosuwaado pazuru ya Hoka no zunou Toreeningu ga Suki Desu.

I love to read and write poetry.
詩を読んだり書いたりするのが大好きです
Shi wo yondari Kaitari suru no Ga daisuki Desu.

My favorite hobby is woodworking and carpentry.
私の好きな趣味は、木工や大工仕事です。
Watashi no suki Na shumi wa, Mokkou ya Daiku shigoto Desu.

I like to go to the beach and spend time by the water.
私はビーチに行って、水辺で時間を過ごすのが好きです。
Watashi wa biichi ni itte, mizube de jikan o sugosu no ga suki desu.

I enjoy playing chess and other strategy games.
私はチェスや他の戦略ゲームをプレイするのが楽しいです。
Watashi wa chesu ya hoka no senryaku geemu o purei suru no ga tanoshii desu.

My favorite hobby is birdwatching and observing wildlife.
私の好きな趣味は、鳥の観察や野生動物の観察です。
Watashi no suki na shumi wa, tori no kansatsu ya yasei doubutsu no kansatsu desu.

I enjoy attending festivals and cultural events.
私は祭りや文化イベントに参加するのが楽しいです。
Watashi wa matsuri ya bunka ibento ni sanka suru no ga tanoshii desu.

I love to go to amusement parks and ride roller coasters.
私は遊園地に行ってジェットコースターに乗ることが大好きです。
Watashi wa yuuenchi ni itte jettokoosutaa ni noru koto ga daisuki desu.

My favorite hobby is collecting vinyl records.
私の好きな趣味は、レコードの収集です。
Watashi no suki na shumi wa, rekoodo no shuushuu desu.

I like to go on long road trips and explore new places.
私は長距離のドライブをして新しい場所を探検するのが好きです。
Watashi wa choukyori no doraibu o shite atarashii basho o tanken suru no ga suki desu.

I enjoy hiking and camping in the mountains.
私は山でハイキングやキャンプをするのが楽しいです。
Watashi wa yama de haikingu ya kyanpu o suru no ga tanoshii desu.

My favorite hobby is baking and trying new dessert recipes.
私の好きな趣味は、お菓子作りや新しいデザートのレシピを試すことです。
Watashi no suki na shumi wa, okashi tsukuri ya atarashii dezato no reshipi o tamesu koto desu.

I like to practice meditation and mindfulness.
私は瞑想やマインドフルネスを実践するのが好きです。
Watashi wa meisou ya maindofurunesu o jissen suru no ga suki desu.

I love to go to the zoo and see all the animals.
私は動物園に行って、すべての動物を見ることが大好きです。
Watashi wa doubutsuen ni itte, subete no doubutsu o miru koto ga daisuki desu.

My favorite hobby is studying different languages.
私の好きな趣味は、異なる言語を学ぶことです。
Watashi no suki na shumi wa, kotonaru gengo o manabu koto desu.

I enjoy watching documentaries and learning new things.
私はドキュメンタリーを見ることや新しいことを学ぶことが楽しいです。
Watashi wa dokyumentarii o miru koto ya atarashii koto o manabu koto ga tanoshii desu.

I like to practice yoga and pilates for exercise.
私はエクササイズのためにヨガやピラティスをするのが好きです。
Watashi wa ekusasaizu no tame ni yoga ya piratisu o suru no ga suki desu.

I enjoy going to concerts and listening to live music.
私はコンサートに行って、ライブ音楽を聴くことが楽しいです。
Watashi wa konsaato ni itte, raibu ongaku o kiku koto ga tanoshii desu.

My favorite hobby is doing puzzles and brain teasers.
私の好きな趣味は、パズルや脳トレをすることです。
Watashi no suki na shumi wa, pazuru ya noutore o suru koto desu.

I like to go on bike rides and explore new trails.
私は自転車に乗って新しい道を探検するのが好きです。
Watashi wa Jitensha ni notte Atarashii michi o Tanken suru no ga suki Desu.

I love to read and watch sci-fi and fantasy movies.
私はSFやファンタジーの本を読んだり、映画を見るのが大好きです。
Watashi wa SF ya fantajii no hon o yondari, eiga o miru no ga daisuki desu.

My favorite hobby is playing video games with friends.
私の好きな趣味は、友達とビデオゲームをすることです。
Watashi no Suki na shumi wa, Tomodachi to Bideo geemu o suru Koto Desu.

I like to go to the park and have picnics with my family.
私は公園に行って、家族とピクニックをするのが好きです。
Watashi wa Kouen Ni itte, Kazoku to pikunikku o Suru no ga suki Desu.

I enjoy playing board games and card games.
私はボードゲームやカードゲームをすることが楽しいです。
Watashi wa Boodo geemu ya Kaado Geemu o suru koto Ga tanoshii Desu.

I like to go to the park and have picnics with my family.
私は家族と公園でピクニックするのが好きです。
Watashi wa kazoku to Kōen de Pikunikku suru no ga suki Desu.

I enjoy playing board games and card games.
私はボードゲームやカードゲームをするのが楽しいです。
Watashi wa Bōdo Gēmu ya kādo gēmu o Suru no ga tanoshii Desu.

My favorite hobby is watching the sunset and taking photographs.

私の好きな趣味は夕日を見て写真を撮ることです

Watashi no suki na Shumi wa yuuhi O mite shashin o Toru koto Desu.

I like to go to museums and learn about art and history.

私は美術館に行って、芸術や歴史について学ぶのが好きです。

Watashi wa Bijutsukan Ni itte, Geijutsu ya Rekishi ni tsuite manabu No ga suki Desu.

I love to cook and experiment with new recipes in the kitchen.

私は料理することが大好きで、新しいレシピを試すのが好きです。

Watashi wa ryōri Suru koto ga daisuki de, Atarashii reshipi o Tamesu no ga Suki Desu.

My favorite hobby is playing the piano and composing music.

私の好きな趣味はピアノを弾いて音楽を作ることです。

Watashi no Suki na shumi wa Piano o hiite ongaku o Tsukuru koto Desu.

I like to go to the beach and swim in the ocean.

私は海岸に行って、海で泳ぐのが好きです。

Watashi wa Kaigan Ni itte, umi de Oyogu no Ga suki Desu.

I enjoy doing outdoor activities like hiking and camping.

私はハイキングやキャンプなどのアウトドア活動が好きです。

Watashi wa Haikingu ya Kyanpu nado no Autodoa katsudō ga suki Desu.

My favorite hobby is collecting rare books and first editions.

私の好きな趣味は、珍しい本や初版を集めることです。

Watashi no suki na Shumi wa, Mezurashii Hon ya shohan o Atsumeru koto Desu.

I like to travel and experience different cultures and cuisines.

私は旅行して、異なる文化や料理を体験するのが好きです。

Watashi wa ryokou Shite, kotonaru Bunka ya ryouri o taiken Suru no ga suki Desu.

I enjoy practicing yoga and meditation for relaxation.
私はリラックスするためにヨガや瞑想をするのが好きです。
Watashi wa Rirakkusu Suru tame ni yoga ya Meiso o suru no Ga suki Desu.

My favorite hobby is horseback riding and taking care of horses.
私のお気に入りの趣味は乗馬と馬の世話をすることです。
Watashi no O-ki-ni-i-Ri no Shu-mi wa jo-u-Ba to uma no se-wa wo su-ru Koto Desu.

I like to attend live theater performances and musicals.
生の劇場やミュージカルを観るのが好きです。
Nama no Geki-jo ya Myu-ji-ka-ru Wo mi-ru no Ga su-ki Desu.

I love to watch and play sports, especially basketball.
スポーツを見たり、特にバスケットボールをするのが大好きす
Su-po-Tsu wo mi-Ta-ri, to-kuni Ba-su-ke-tto-Bo-ru wo su-ru no Ga dai-su-ki Desu.

# MAKING PLANS

What are you up to this weekend?
今週末に何をしているのですか？
Konshuumatsu ni Nani o shiteiru no Desu ka?

Let's make plans for Saturday.
土曜日の計画を立てましょう。
Doyoubi No keikaku o tatemashou.

How about we grab dinner on Friday?
金曜日にディナーを食べに行きませんか？
Kinyoubi ni dinā O tabe ni ikimasen ka?

Are you free on Saturday afternoon?
土曜日の午後は空いていますか？
Doyoubi no gogo wa aiteimasu ka?

Let's get together sometime this week.
今週のうちに会いましょう。
Konshuu no Uchi ni Aimashou.

What's your availability like next week?
来週の予定はどうですか？
Raishuu No yotei Wa dou Desu ka?

Can we schedule a time to meet up?
会う時間をスケジュールできますか？
Au jikan o Sukejuuru Dekimasu ka?

Let's plan something fun for next weekend.
来週末に楽しいことを計画しましょう。
Raishuumatsu ni Tanoshii koto o keikaku Shimashou.

How about we go for a hike on Sunday?
日曜日にハイキングに行きませんか？
Nichiyoubi ni Haikingu ni Ikimasen ka?

Let's plan a road trip for next month.
来月にロードトリップを計画しましょう。
Raigetsu ni Roodo Torippu o keikaku Shimashou.

Would you like to join us for drinks tonight?
今晩一緒に飲みに行きませんか？
Konban Issho ni Nomi Ni Ikimasen ka?

Let's catch up over coffee this week.
今週中にコーヒーで話しましょう。
What's your Schedule like for Next weekend?

Let's make a reservation for Friday night.
金曜日の夜の予約をしましょう。
Kinyoubi no yoru no yoyaku o Shimashou.

How about we plan a picnic for Sunday?
日曜日にピクニックを計画しましょう。
Nichiyoubi ni Pikunikku o Keikaku Shimashou.

Let's organize a movie night this weekend.
今週末に映画の夜を企画しましょう。
Konshuumatsu Ni eiga no yoru o Kikaku Shimashou.

Would you like to come to a party on Saturday?
土曜日にパーティーに来ませんか？
Doyoubi ni Paatii ni Kimasen ka?

How about we have a game night this Friday?
今週の金曜日にゲームの夜をしましょうか？
Konshuu no Kinyoubi ni ge-Mu no yoru o Shimashou ka?

Let's plan a road trip for next month.
来月、ドライブ旅行を計画しましょう。
Raigetsu, Doraibu ryokou Okeikaku Shimashou.

What are your plans for the weekend?
週末の予定は何ですか？
Shuumatsu no yotei wa nan desu ka?

Would you like to grab a coffee sometime?
いつかコーヒーでも飲みに行きませんか？
Itsuka koohii Demo nomi Ni ikimasen ka?

Would you like to join me?
私と一緒に参加しませんか？
Watashi to issho ni sanka shimasen ka?

How about we catch a movie later?
後で映画でも見に行きましょうか？
Ato de eiga demo mi ni ikimashou ka?

Let's plan a dinner party next week
来週、夕食会を計画しましょう。
Raishuu, yuushoku-Kai O keikaku Shimashou.

What day works for you?
どの日があなたにとって都合がいいですか？
Dono hi ga Anata ni totte Tsugou ga ii Desu ka?

I was thinking we could go to the beach.
海に行ってみたらどうですか？
Umi ni itte Mitara dou Desu ka?

Do you want to grab lunch together tomorrow?
明日一緒にランチしませんか？
Ashita issho Ni Ranchi Shimasen ka?

Morgen samen lunchen?
明日一緒にランチしませんか？
Ashita issho ni Ranchi Shimasen ka?

Do you want to grab lunch together tomorrow?
> 明日一緒にランチしませんか？
Ashita issho ni RANCHI shimasen ka?

Morgen samen lunchen?
> 明日一緒にランチしませんか？
Ashita issho ni RANCHI shimasen ka?

Do you want to try it out this weekend?
> 今週末に試してみたいですか？
Konshuumatsu ni Tameshite Mitai desu ka?

Let's plan a hiking trip soon.
> 近いうちにハイキングの旅行を計画しましょう。
Chikai uchi ni HAIKINGU no Ryokou o keikaku Shimashou.

What trail do you want to go to?
> どのトレイルに行きたいですか？
Dono TOREIRU ni ikitai desu ka?

Are you interested in attending this concert next month?
> 来月のコンサートに興味ありますか？
Raigetsu no KONSAATO ni kyoumi Arimasu ka?

# TALKING ABOUT DAILY ROUTINES

What time do you wake up?
何時に起きますか？
Nanji ni Okimasu ka?

Do you have a morning routine?
朝のルーティンはありますか？
Asa no rutin wa Arimasu ka?

Do you exercise daily?
毎日運動をしますか？
Mainichi undou o Shimasu ka?

What time do you go to bed?
何時に寝ますか？
Nanji ni nemasu ka?

What's your favorite part of your daily routine?
日課の中で一番好きな部分は何ですか？
Nikka no naka De ichiban suki na Bubun wa Nanidesu ka?

Do you have any daily hobbies or activities?
日常的な趣味や活動はありますか？
Nichijouteki Na shumi ya Katsudou wa Arimasu ka?

Would you like to change anything about your daily routine?
日課に何か変えたいことはありますか？
Nikka ni Nanika Kaetai Koto wa Arimasu ka?

I commute to work/school.
通勤/通学します。
Tsuukin/tsuugaku Shimasu.

I take a walk during my lunch break.
昼休みに散歩します。
Hiruyasumi Ni sanpo Shimasu.

I continue working/studying in the afternoon.
午後も仕事/勉強を続けます。
Gogo mo shigoto/Benkyou o Tsuzukemasu.

I have a snack in the afternoon.
午後におやつを食べます。
Gogo ni Oyatsu o Tabemasu.

I commute back home.
帰宅します。
Kitaku Shimasu.

I read a book in the evening.
夜に本を読みます。
Yoru ni hon o yomimasu.

I take a bath or shower before bed.
寝る前にお風呂またはシャワーを浴びます。
Neru mae ni Ofuro Matawa shawaa o Abimasu.

I brush my teeth before bed.
寝る前に歯を磨きます。
 Neru mae ni ha o migakimasu.

I go to bed at...
...に寝ます。
...Ni Nemasu.

I fall asleep quickly.
すぐに眠りにつきます。
Sugu ni Nemuri ni Tsukimasu.

I wake up in the middle of the night.
夜中に目が覚めます。
Yonaka ni me ga samemasu.

I have trouble falling back to sleep.
再び眠りにつくのが難しいです。
Futatabi nemuri ni tsuku no ga muzukashii desu.

# GIVING AND ASKING FOR ADVICE

In my opinion, you should...
私の意見では、あなたは
Watashi no Iken dewa, Anata wa

From my experience, I would recommend that you...
私の経験から、おすすめするのは
Watashi no Keiken kara, Osusume suru No wa

If I were in your shoes, I would...
もし私があなたなら、私は
Moshi watashi ga Anata nara, Watashi wa

One possible solution could be...
ひとつの解決策は
Hitotsu no Kaiketsusaku wa

I think it would be a good idea to...
良いアイデアだと思います。
Yoi aidea Da to Omoimasu

Why don't you try...
してみたらどうですか？
Shite Mitara dou Desu ka?

It might be helpful to...
役に立つかもしれません
Yaku Ni tatsu Kamoshiremasen

What do you think I should do?
私に何をすべきかと思いますか？
Watashi ni nani wo Subeki ka to Omoimasu ka?

Can you give me some advice on this?
これについてアドバイスをくれますか？
Kore Ni tsuite adobaisu Go Kuremasu ka?

I'm not sure what to do, can you help me out?
何をすべきかわからないので、手伝ってもらえますか？
Nani wo Subeki ka wakaranai Node, tetsudatte Moraemasu ka?

Do you have any suggestions for me?
私に何か提案はありますか？
Watashi ni nanika teian wa Arimasu ka?

What would you do in my situation?
私の状況だったら、あなたは何をしますか？
Watashi No joukyou dattara, Anata wa nani wo Shimasu ka?

Could you give me your opinion on this matter?
この件についてあなたの意見をお聞かせいただけますか？
Kono ken ni tsuite Nata no iken wo Okikaseitadakemasu ka?

What's your take on this?
この件について、あなたの見解は何ですか？
Kono ken ni tsuite, anata no kenkai wa Nanidesu ka?

Can you offer any insights on this issue?
この問題について何か知見を提供できますか？
Kono Mondai ni tsuite Nanika Chiken wo teikyou Dekimasu ka?

I'd appreciate your input on this.
これについてあなたの意見を聞きたいと思います。
Kore ni tsuite Anata no iken Wo kikitai to Omoimasu.

Do you have any recommendations?
何かおすすめはありますか？
Nanika osusume Wa arimasu Ka?

What's your advice on how to handle this?
どう対処したらいいか、あなたのアドバイスを教えてください。
Dou taisho shitara ii ka, Anata no adobaisu wo Oshiete kudasai.

Can you share any wisdom on this topic?
このトピックに関するあなたの知恵を教えていただけますか？
Kono Topikku ni kansuru Anata no chie wo Oshiete itadakemasu ka?

I'm seeking some guidance, can you point me in the right direction?
何か指導がほしいので、適切な方向を指示していただけますか？
Nanika shidou Ga hoshii node, Tekisetsu na Houkou wo shiji Shite itadakemasu ka?

I think you should...
あなたは...するべきだと思います。
Anata wa ... Suru beki da to Omoimasu.

My advice would be to...
私のアドバイスは...です。
Watashi no Adobaisu wa ... Desu.

If I were you, I would...
もし私があなたなら、...するでしょう。
Moshi watashi ga Anata nara, ... suru Deshou.

What do you think I should do?
私には何をすべきだと思いますか？
Watashi ni wa nani wo Subeki da to Omoimasu ka?

Can you give me some advice on...? ...
についてアドバイスをくれますか？
... Ni tsuite adobaisu wo Kuremasu ka?

I'm not sure what to do, what would you suggest?
何をすべきかわからないので、何か提案はありますか？
Nani wo subeki ka wakaranai node, Nanika teian wa Arimasu ka?

# TALKING ABOUT LIKES AND DISLIKES

I enjoy spending time with them.
彼らと一緒に過ごすのが楽しいです。
Karera to Issho ni sugosu no Ga tanoshii Desu.

I really like it.
私はそれが本当に好きです。
Watashi wa sore ga Hontō ni suki desu.

I'm a big fan of it.
私はそれの大ファンです。
Watashi wa Sore no dai fan Desu.

I'm fond of it.
私はそれが好きです。
Watashi wa Sore ga suki Desu.

It's one of my favorites.
それは私のお気に入りの一つです。
Sore wa Watashi no Kiniiri no hitotsu Desu.

I enjoy it.
私はそれを楽しんでいます。
Watashi wa sore wo tanoshinde imasu.

It's right up my alley.
それは私の好みにぴったりです
Sore wa watashi No konomi ni Pittari Desu.

It's right up my street.
それは私の通りにぴったりです
Sore wa Watashi no tōri ni Pittari Desu.

I'm not a fan of it.
それは私のファンではない。
Sore wa Watashi no FAN de Wa nai

It doesn't appeal to me.
私には魅力的ではない。
Watashi ni wa Miryokuteki de Wa nai

It's not my thing.
私のタイプではない。
Watashi no TAIPU de Wa nai

It's a turn-off for me.
私にとってはドン引きだ。
Watashi ni Totte wa Donbiki da

I find it unpleasant.
私にとって不快だ。
Watashi Ni totte Fukai da

It bothers me.
私を悩ませる。
Watashi wo Nayamaseru

It rubs me the wrong way.
私を不快にさせる。
Watashi wo fukai ni Saseru

# EXPRESSING AGREEMENT OR DISAGREEMENT

I agree with you.
あなたに同意します。
Anata ni Doui Shimasu

That's exactly what I was thinking.
正に私が思っていたことです。
Tadashii ni watashi Ga omotte Ita koto Desu

I couldn't have said it better myself.
私自身、それ以上上手く言えませんでした。
Watashi jishin, Sore ijou umaku Iemasen Deshita

I see your point.
あなたの言いたいことは分かります。
Anata no iitai Koto wa Wakarimasu

You're absolutely right.
あなたは完全に正しいです。
Anata wa kanzen Ni tadashii Desu

I couldn't agree with you more.
もっと同意できないくらいです。
Motto doui Dekinai kurai Desu

That makes perfect sense to me.
それは完璧に理解できます。
Sore wa kanpeki Ni rikai Dekimasu

I see things the same way.
私も同じように考えます。
Watashi mo Nnaji you ni Kangaemasu

You're spot on.
まさにその通りです。
masa ni sono doori desu

I see where you're coming from, but I disagree.
あなたの言い分は分かりますが、私は反対です。
Anata no iibun wa Wakarimasu ga, watashi wa Hantai Desu

I'm not sure I agree with that.
私はそれに同意できるかどうか分かりません。
Watashi wa Sore ni doui Dekiru ka Dou ka Wakarimasen

I'm not convinced.
私は納得していません。
Watashi wa Nattoku shite Imasen

I'm afraid I don't agree with you.
残念ですが、私はあなたに同意できません。
zannen desu ga, watashi wa anata ni doui dekimasen

That's not how I see it.
私の見方とは異なります。
Watashi no Mikata to wa Kotonari Masu

I respectfully disagree.
敬意を持って反対意見を述べます。
Keii wo Motte hantai iken wo Nobemasu

That's not my understanding.
私の理解ではそうではありません。
Watashi no rikai Dewa sou De wa Arimasen

## MAKING EXCUSES

I'm sorry, I can't make it to the meeting tomorrow.
めんなさい、明日のミーティングには参加できません。
Go-men-na-sai, A-shi-ta-no mi-i-Tin-gu-ni-wa San-ka-de-ki-ma-Sen

I wish I could help, but I'm already swamped with work.
手伝いたいのですが、仕事で忙しくてできません。
Te-tsu-da-I-tai-no-de-su-Ga, shi-goto-De-isogashi-ku-Te-de-ki-ma-Sen

I'm sorry, but I won't be able to stay for the whole event.
申し訳ありませんが、イベントの最後まで居られません。
Mo-shi-wa-Ke-a-ri-Ma-sen-ga,
i-be-n-to-No-sai-go-ma-De-i-ra-re-ma-Sen

I wish I could come.
行けるといいんですが。
I-ke-ru-To-i-i-n-de-su-Ga

Unfortunately, I already have plans that night.
残念ですが、その日はすでに予定があります。
Zan-nen-de-su-Ga, so-No-hi-wa-su-De-ni-yo-tei-ga-A-ri-ma-Su

I'm sorry, but I have to work late that day.
その日は遅くまで仕事をしなければなりません。
So-no-hi-wa-O-so-ku-ma-de-shi-Go-to-shi-na-Ke-re-ba-na-ri-Ma-se-N

I'm sorry, but I have a conflict that day.
申し訳ありませんが、その日に予定が重なっています。
Mo-shi-wa-ke-a-ri-ma-sen-Ga,
so-no-hi-ni-yo-tei-ga-ka-sa-Na-tte-i-ma-Su

I'm sorry, but I have a prior commitment.
申し訳ありませんが、先約があります。
Mo-shi-wa-ke-A-ri-Ma-sen-ga, Sen-yaku-ga-a-ri-ma-Su

Unfortunately, I won't be able to make it.
残念ですが、参加できません。
Zan-nen-De-su-ga, San-ka-de-ki-ma-Sen

I'm really sorry, but I have to attend to something else.
本当に申し訳ありませんが、他の用事があります。
Hon-to-ni-mo-shi-Wa-ke-a-ri-Ma-sen-Ga, ta-no-yo-u-ji-Ga-a-ri-ma-Su

I apologize, but I won't be able to attend.
申し訳ありませんが、出席できません。
Mo-shi-wa-ke-a-Ri-ma-sen-Ga, shus-seki-De-ki-ma-Sen

I'm sorry, but I'm not feeling well and won't be able to attend.
ごめんなさい、調子が悪くて参加できません。
Go-men-na-sai, Cho-u-shi-ga-wa-ku-Te-san-ka-De-ki-ma-Sen

I'm sorry, but I already made other plans for that day.
申し訳ありませんが、その日は別の予定が入っています
Mo-shi-wa-ke-A-ri-ma-sen-Ga,
so-no-Hi-wa-be-Tsu-no-yo-Tei-ga-hai-ru-Te-i-ma-Su

I'm afraid I won't be able to come because of personal reasons.
個人的な理由で参加できない恐れがあります。
Ko-jin-te-ki-na-ri-yuu-De-san-ka-de-ki-Na-i-osore-ga-a-ri-Ma-su

I'm sorry, but I have a doctor's appointment that day.
申し訳ありませんが、その日は医師の予約が入っています。
Mo-shi-wa-ke-a-ri-Ma-sen-ga,
so-No-hi-wa-i-Shi-no-yo-yaku-ga-hai-Ru-te-i-ma-S

I'm sorry, but I have a doctor's appointment that day.
ごめんなさいが、その日はお医者さんの予約があるので
go-meh-nah-sigh-Gah,
Sono-hi-wa-o-Ee-Sha-san-No-yoyaku-gah-ah-Ru-no-De

I apologize, but I have unexpected circumstances to deal with.
申し訳ありませんが、予期せぬ事態が発生したので
Mo-shi-wah-keh-Ah-ree-mah-sen-Gah,yo-ki-seh-Nu-ji-tai-gah-Hah-tsu-
oh-shi-ta-No-De

I'm afraid I won't be able to attend due to a personal emergency.
　残念ですが、個人的な緊急事態が起こってしまったので
Zahn-nen-deh-suh-Gah,koh-Jin-teh-kee-Nah-kin-kyuu-ji-Tai-gah-o-Koht
-teh-shi-Mah-tah-no-De

I'm sorry, but I have a prior engagement that I can't cancel.
申し訳ありませんが、キャンセルできない別の予定があるため
Mo-shi-wah-keh-ah-ree-Mah-sen-gah,kyahn-sell-Deh-ki-nah-ee-Beh-ts
u-no-yo-tei-gah-Ah-ru-tah-Meh

I'm sorry, but I have to take care of my pet that day.
申し訳ありませんが、その日はペットの世話をしなければなら
ないので
Mo-shi-wah-keh-ah-ree-Mah-sen-gah,sono-hi-Wa-Peh-tto-no-Seh-wa-
wo-Shi-Nah-keh-reh-Bah-Nah-rah-nai-No-De

I'm afraid I can't attend due to transportation issues.
　残念ですが、交通の問題があって出席できない可能性がありま
す
Zahn-nen-Deh-suh-gah,Koh-toh-no-Mohn-dai-gah-ah-Tte-shus-seh-ki-
Nah-ee-kah-noh-Oh-poh-see-Gah-ah-ri-Mahs

I'm sorry, but I have a work obligation that day.
申し訳ありませんが、その日は仕事の義務がありますので
Mo-shi-wahKkeh-ah-Ree-mah-Sen-Gah,sono-Hi-wa-shee-Goh-no-gi-m
oo-Gah-ah-Ree-mahs-noh-Deh

I apologize, but I simply can't make it that day.
申し訳ありませんが、単純にその日は参加できませ
Mo-shi-Wah-keh-ah-ree-Mah-sen-gah,Tan-jyuu-ni-Sono-hi-wa-san-ka-
deh-ki-Mah-sen

## ASKING AND GIVING PERMISSION

Is it okay if I leave work early today?
今日、仕事を早退してもいいですか？
Kyou, Shigoto wo SoutaIshIte Mo ii Desu Ka?

Can I use your computer for a few minutes?
ちょっとだけ、あなたのコンピューターを使ってもいいですか？
Chotto dake, Anata no Konpyuutaawo tsukatte mo ii Desu ka?

Can I borrow your pen, please?
ペンを借りてもいいですか？
Pen wo karitete mo ii desu ka?

May I use the restroom?
トイレを使ってもいいですか？
Toire wo tsukattemo ii desu ka?

Could I leave work a bit early today?
今日は少し早く退社してもいいですか？
Kyou wa Sukoshi HaYaku TaiSha shitemo ii Desu ka?

Would it be okay if I took a day off next week?
来週、1日休んでもいいですか？
Raishuu, Ichinichi yasundemo ii Desu ka?

Is it alright if I take a photo of this painting?
この絵を写真に撮ってもいいですか？
Kono E wo shashin Ni tottemo Ii Desu ka?

Can I speak with your supervisor, please?
上司と話してもいいですか？
Joushi to Hanashitemo Ii desu ka?

May I have your permission to share this information?
この情報を共有してもいいですか？
Kono jouhou wo kyouyuu Shitemo ii Desu ka?

Would it be possible for me to borrow your car?
車を借りてもいいですか？
Kuruma wo karitete mo ii desu ka?

Do you mind if I turn on the air conditioning?
エアコンをつけてもいいですか？
Eakon wo Tsuketemo Ii Desu ka?

Is it okay if I invite a friend to dinner tonight?
今晩、友達を夕食に招待してもいいですか？
Konban, Tomodachi wo Uushoku ni Shoutai shitemo Ii desu ka?

Can I use your phone for a quick call?
短い電話をかけてもいいですか？
Mijikai denwa wo Kakete mo Ii desu ka?

Would you allow me to bring my dog inside?
犬を中に入れてもいいですか？
Inu wo naka ni iretemo ii desu ka?

May I have your permission to use this photograph in my presentation?
プレゼンテーションでこの写真を使ってもいいですか？
Purezenteesshon de Kono Shashin wo Tsukattemo Ii Desu ka?

Can I leave my coat here while I run errands?
用事を済ませる間、コートをここに置いておいてもいいですか？
Youji wo Sumaseru Aida, Koto wo koko ni Oite oitemo ii Desu ka?

# MAKING COMPARISONS

How does this compare to that?
これは、あれと比べてどうですか？
Kore Wa, are to Kurabete Dou desu ka?

Which one do you think is better?
どちらが良いと思いますか？
Dochira Ga yoi to Omoimasu ka?

In what ways are these two things alike or different?
これらの2つのものは、どのように似ていますか、または異なっ
ていますか？
Kore Ra no futatsu No mono wa, Dono you ni nite Imasu ka, Mata wa
kotonatte Imasu ka?

Which one do you prefer, X or Y?
とYのどちらが好きですか？
X to Y no Dochira Ga suki Gesu ka?

What are the advantages and disadvantages of each option?
各オプションの利点と欠点は何ですか？
Kaku Opushon no Riten to ketten wa Nanidesu ka?

What are the pros and cons of each alternative?
各選択肢の利点と欠点は何ですか？
Kaku sentakushi no riten to ketten wa nanidesu ka?

# EXPRESSING GRATITUDE AND APOLOGIES

Thank you so much!
どうもありがとうございます
Domo arigatou Gozaimasu

Thanks for being there for me.
いつもそばにいてくれてありがとう
Itsumo soba Ni ite kurete Arigatou

I can't thank you enough.
感謝の気持ちでいっぱいです
Kansha No kimochi de Ippai desu

Thank you for your kindness.
優しさに感謝します
Yasashisa Ni kansha Shimasu

Thank you from the bottom of my heart.
心から感謝しています
Kokoro kara Kansha shite Imasu

Thanks a million!
何十万回もありがとう
Nanjuu man Kai mo Arigatou

I'm sorry.
ごめんなさい
Gomen Nasai

I apologize.
謝罪します
Shazai Shimasu

Please forgive me.
許してください
Yurushite Kudasai

I take full responsibility.
責任を取ります
Sekinin O Torimasu

I regret my actions.
行動を後悔しています
Koudou O koukai Shite Imasu

I didn't mean to hurt you.
傷つけるつもりはありませんでした
Kizutsukeru tsumori wa Arimasen Deshita

I promise to make it up to you.
言い訳をせずに取り戻します
Iiwake o Sezu Ni Torimodoshi Masu

I understand if you don't forgive me.
許してもらえないことも理解しています
Yurushite Moraenai Koto mo rikai Shite Imasu

I really appreciate your help.
本当に助けられました
Hontou ni Tasukerare Mashita

I can't thank you enough for what you've done.
あなたがしてくれたことに感謝しきれません
Anata ga shite kureta koto ni kansha Shikiremasen

You have my sincere gratitude.
心から感謝しています
Kokoro kara Kansha shite Imasu

I'm so grateful for your kindness.
あなたの優しさに感謝しています
Anata no yasashisa Ni kansha Simasu

I'm truly thankful for your support.
あなたのサポートに本当に感謝しています。
Anata no sa-po-to ni Hon-Tou ni kan-Sha shi-te i-Masu.

I can't express how grateful I am.
私はどれだけ感謝しているか表現できません。
Watashi wa DO-re da-ke kan-Sha shi-te i-ru ka Hyoo-gen de-ki-ma-Sen.

I'm indebted to you for your generosity.
あなたの寛大さにはお礼が言い尽くせません。
Anata no kan-DAI-sa ni wa o-REI ga i-i-tsu-ku se-ma-Sen.

I'm blessed to have you in my life.
私はあなたが人生にいることを幸せに思います。
Watashi wa anata Ga jin-sei ni iru Koto wo shi-Awa-se ni o-mo-i-Masu.

Your help has been invaluable to me.
あなたの助けは私にとって非常に貴重でした。
Anata no ta-su-ke Wa watashi ni tot-te HI-Joo-ni ki-chou De-shi-ta.

You're a true lifesaver, thank you.
あなたは本当の命の恩人です、ありがとう。
Anata wa Hon-Tou no i-no-ri no on-jin De-su, a-ri-Ga-to-U.

I'll never forget your kindness.
あなたの親切を決して忘れません。
Anata no shin-setsu wo ke-She-te Wa-su-re-ma-se-N.

I'm so fortunate to have you as a friend.
あなたを友達に持てることがとても幸運だと思います。
Anata wo to-mo-da-chi ni mo-te-ru koto ga to-te-mo ko-u-n de to o-mo-i-ma
su.

Your assistance means the world to me.
あなたの援助は私にとって世界中のものです。
Anata no En-jo wa watashi ni tot-te SekAI-juu no Mono De-su.

I'm touched by your thoughtfulness.
あなたの思いやりに感動しています。
Anata no o-mo-i-ya-ri Ni kan-Doo shi-te i-masu.

# MAKING PHONE CALLS

Hello, this is [your name].
もしもし、[your name] です。
Mo-shi-mo-shi, [ ] De-su.

May I speak to [name of the person]?
[person's name] さんをお願いします。
[ ] san wo o-NE-gai shi-Masu.

May I have your name and telephone number, please?
お名前と電話番号を教えていただけますか？
O-na-ma-e to Den-wa Ban-go wo O-shie-te i-ta-da-ke-Ma-Su ka?

Could you call me back?
折り返し電話をしていただけますか？
O-ri-kae-shi Den-wa wo shi-te i-ta-Da-ke-ma-Su ka?

Hello, can I speak with...? ...
さんとお話してもよろしいですか？
...San to o-ha-Na-Shi shi-te Mo yo-ro-shi-i De-su ka?

Hello, is...available? ...
さんはいらっしゃいますか？
...San wa i-ra-Sshai-Ma-su ka?

May I know who I'm speaking with?
お名前をお聞きしてもよろしいですか？
O-Na-ma-e wo o-ki-ki Shi-te mo yo-No-shi-i De-su ka?

I'm sorry, you have the wrong number.
申し訳ありませんが、番号が間違っています。
Mo-shi-wa-ke a-ri-Ma-sen-ga, Ban-go ga ma-cha-kot-te i-Ma-su.

Can I take a message?
メッセージをお伝えしてもよろしいでしょうか？
Me-Sse-ji wo O-tsu-tae Si-te mo yo-ro-shi-i de-shou Ka?

Please hold the line for a moment.
少々お待ちください。
Shou-shou o-ma-tsu-ki ku-da-sai.

I'll transfer your call.
お電話をおつなぎいたします。
O-den-wa Wo o-tsu-na-gi-i-ta-Shi-masu.

Let me check
確認{かくにん}してみます
Kaku-Nin shi-te Mi-mas

I'll check to see if he/she is available
彼{かれ} / 彼女{かのじょ}がいるか確認{かくにん}してみます
ka-Re / ka-No-jo ga i-ru ka kaku-Nin shi-te Mi-mas

# DESCRIBING FEELINGS AND EMOTIONS

I feel happy.
私はしあわせなきもち
Watashi wa Shiawase Na Kimochi

I feel sad.
私はかなしいきもち
Watashi wa Kanashii Kimochi

I feel angry.
私はおこっているきもち
Watashi wa Okotte iru Kimochi

I feel anxious.
私はあんしんできないきもち
Watashi wa Anshin dekinai Kimochi

I feel nervous.
私はどきどきするきもち
Watashi wa Dokidoki suru Kimochi

I feel scared.
私はこわがるきもち
Watashi wa Kowagaru Kimochi

I feel excited.
私はわくわくするきもち
Watashi wa Wakuwaku Suru Kimochi

I feel overwhelmed.
私はあふれるきもち
Watashi wa Afureru Kimochi

I feel content.
私はもうけんきなきもち
Watashi wa Mōkenki na Kimochi

I feel frustrated.
私はイライラするきもち
Watashi wa Iraira Suru Kimochi

I feel disappointed.
私はがっかりするきもち
Watashi wa Gakkari Suru Kimochi

I feel lonely.
私はさびしいきもち
Watashi Wa sabishii Kimochi

I feel loved.
私はあいされているきもち
Watashi wa Aisarete Iru Kimochi

I feel appreciated.
私はかんしゃされているきもち
watashi wa kansha sarete iru kimochi

I feel grateful.
私はかんしゃしているきもち
Watashi wa Kansha Shite iru Kimochi

I feel jealous.
私はやきもちをやいているきもち
Watashi Wyakimochi Wo yaite Iru Kimochi

I feel envious.
私はうらやむきもち
Watashi wa Urayamu Kimochi

I feel guilty.
私はざんねんなきもち
Watashi wa Zannen na Kimochi

149

I feel ashamed.
私ははずかしいきもち
Watashi wa Hazukashii Kimochi

I feel proud.
私はほこりをかんじるきもち
Watashi wa Hokori wo Kanjiru Kimochi

I feel confident.
私はじしんがあるきもち
Watashi wa Jishin ga aru Kimochi

I feel insecure.
私はあんぜんでないきもち
Watashi wa Anzen De nai Kimochi

I feel inferior.
私はにげんじょうきもち
Watashi wa Nigenjō Kimochi

I feel superior.
私はじょうようじょうきもち
Watashi Wa Jōyōjō Kimochi

I feel relaxed.
私はりらっくすしたきもち
Watashi Wa Rirakkusu Shita Kimochi

I feel relaxed.
リラックスしています。
Ri-ra-ku-Su shi-te i-Masu

I feel exhausted.
疲れ果てています。
Tsukare-ha-te-Te i-masu

I feel energized.
エネルギッシュです。
E-ne-ru-Gi-shu Desu

I feel motivated.
やる気が出ています。
Ya-ru-ki ga De-te i-Masu

I feel inspired.
インスピレーションを感じています。
In-su-Pi-re-shon Wo ka-nji-te i-Masu

I feel bored.
退屈しています。
Tai-kutsu Shi-Te i-masu

How are you feeling today?
今日はどんな気分ですか？
Kyo wa Don-na ki-Bun Desu ka?

What's been bothering/upsetting you lately?
最近、何か心配事や不安なことがありますか？
Saikin, Nanika Shinpai-ji ya Fuan-na koto Ga a-ri-Masu ka?

Are you feeling anxious/nervous about something in particular?
特定のことで不安や緊張を感じていますか？
Tokutei No koto De fuan ya kin-Chou Wo kan-ji-Te i-masu ka?

Have you been experiencing any strong emotions recently?
最近、強い感情を感じたことはありますか？
Saikin, Tsuyo-i kan-Jou wo kan-jit-a koto Wa a-ri-Masu ka?

Have you experienced strong emotions lately?
最近{さいきん}、強{つよ}い感情{かんじょう}を感{かん}じたことがありますか？
Sa-i-kin, tsu-YO-i KAN-jyo wo KAN-ji-ta ko-to ga a-ri-Mas ka?

151

Is there anything that's been making you feel happy/joyful lately?
最近、何か嬉しいことがありましたか？
Saikin, Nanika ureshii koto Ga a-ri-Mashita ka?

How do you feel about the current situation?
現在の状況についてどう思いますか？
Gen-zai no jou-kyou ni tsui-te Dou omoi-Masu ka?

Are you comfortable talking about your feelings with me?
私と感情について話すのは心地よいですか？
Watashi to kan-jou ni tsui-Te Hanasu no wa Kokochi-yoi Desu ka?

Would you like to discuss how you're feeling in more detail?
もっと詳しく気持ちについて話したいですか？
Motto Kuwashiku Kimochi Ni Tsuite Hanashi-Tai Desu ka?

# DISCUSSING HEALTH AND WELL-BEING

I'm feeling great today!
今日は調子がいいです！
Kyo wa Choushi Ga ii Desu!

I've been really tired lately and need to get more sleep.
最近疲れていて、もっと睡眠を取る必要があります。
Saikin Tsukarete ite, Motto suimin Wo toru Hitsuyou ga Arimasu.

I need to start exercising more regularly.
もっと定期的に運動を始める必要があります。
Motto teikiteki ni Undou wo Hajimeru Hitsuyou ga Arimasu.

I've been eating healthier and feel much better.
より健康的な食事をしていて、体調が良くなっています。
Yori kenkouteki na Shokuji wo Shite ite, Taichou Ga yoku natte Imasu.

I'm trying to cut back on sugar and processed foods.
砂糖や加工食品を減らすようにしています。
Satou ya Kakou Shokuhin wo Herasu you ni Shite Imasu.

I've been struggling with anxiety and am seeking help.
不安に悩んでおり、助けを求めています。
Fuan ni nayande ori, tasuke wo motomete imasu.

I think I'm coming down with a cold.
風邪{かぜ}を引{ひ}いたかもしれない。
ka-ze wo Hi-i-ta ka-Mo she-re-Nai

I'm recovering from an injury and need to take it easy for a while.
けがをしたので、しばらくはゆっくりする必要{ひつよう}があり
ます。
Ga wo shi-Ta no de, shi-ba-Ra-ku wa yuk-ku-ri Su-ru hi-Tsu-yo-u ga
A-ri-ma-Su

I'm trying to quit smoking for my health.
健康{けんこう}のために、禁煙{きんえん}を試{ため}みています。
Ken-kou no Ta-me ni, Kin-en wo ta-Me-mi-te i-ma-Su

I've been having trouble sleeping and need to talk to my doctor about it.
眠{ねむ}りにくくて、医者{いしゃ}に相談{そうだん}する必要が あります。
Ne-mu-ri ni-ku-ku-te, i-Sha ni sou-Dan su-ru Hi-tsu-yo-u Ga a-ri-ma-Su

I've been feeling down lately and think I might be depressed.
最近{さいきん}気分{きぶん}が落{お}ち込{こ}んでいて、うつ病{ぶつびょう}かもしれないと 思{おも}っています。
Sai-kin ki-bun Ga o-Chi-ko-n De i-te, Bu-tsu-Byo-u ka-Mo She-re-nai to o-Mo-tte i-ma-Su

I'm trying to lose weight for my overall health.
全体{ぜんたい}的{てき}な健康{けんこう}のために、体重{たいじゅう}を減{へ}らすようにしています。
Zen-tai-te-ki-Na ken-kou no ta-Me ni, tai-juu wo He-ra-su you ni Shi-te i-ma-Su

I've been getting more rest and sleep lately to improve my overall well-being.
健康{けんこう}維持{いじ}のために、最近{さいきん}はもっと休{やす}んで寝{ね}るようにしています。
Ken-kou i-ji no Ta-me ni, Sai-kin wa Mot-to yas-un-De ne-ru you Ni shi-te i-ma-Su

I'm going to start seeing a therapist to work on my mental health.
メンタルヘルスの改善{かいぜん}のために、セラピストに通{かよ}うつもりです。
Men-ta-ru Heru-su no Kai-zen no ta-me ni, Se-ra-pi-su-to ni ka-yo-u tu-Mo-ri de-U

I need to go for a check-up with my doctor.
医者{いしゃ}の診察{しんさつ}に行{い}かなければなりません。
I-sha no Shin-sa-Tsu ni i-ka-na-Ke-re-ba na-ri-Ma-Su

I'm trying to drink more water and stay hydrated.

もっと水分{すいぶん}をとって、水分補給{すいぶんほきゅう}に気{き}をつけています。

Mot-to sui-bun wo to-tte, sui-bun ho-kyuu ni ki wo tsu-ke-te i-ma-su

I've been experiencing some digestive issues and need to watch what I eat.

消化{しょうか}に問題{もんだい}があり、食{た}べるものに気{き}をつけなければなりません。

Shou-ka ni Mon-dai ga a-ri, Ta-be-ru mo-No ni ki wo Tsu-ke-na-ke-Re-ba na-ri-ma-Su

I'm taking vitamins to supplement my diet.

食{しょく}事{じ}に補助{ほじょ}的{てき}にビタミンを取{と}っています。

Sho-ku-ji ni Ho-jo-te-Ti ni bi-ta-Min wo to-tte i-Ma-su

I've been feeling more energetic since starting a new exercise routine.

新{あたら}しい運動{うんどう}の習慣{しゅうかん}を始{はじ}めてから、体{からだ}がもっと元気{げんき}になっています。

A-ta-ra-shi-i Un-dou no Shuu-kan wo ha-ji-Me-te ka-ra, ka-ra-Da ga mot-to Gen-ki ni Na-tte i-ma-Su

I'm trying to reduce my alcohol intake for my health.

健康{けんこう}のために、アルコールの摂取{せっしゅ}量{りょう}を減{へ}らすようにしています。

Ken-kou no ta-Me ni, aru-koo-ru No ses-shu-Ryou wo He-ra-su you ni Shi-te i-ma-Su

I'm working on improving my mental clarity and focus.

私は精神的な明晰さと集中力を向上するように取り組んでいます。

Watashi wa seishinteki na Meiseisa to Shuuchuuryoku o Koujou suru you ni Torikumete Imasu.

I need to take a break and relax to reduce my stress levels.
ストレスレベルを下げるために、休憩してリラックスする必要があります。
Sutoresu reberu o Sageru tame ni, kyuukei Shite rirakkusu Suru hitsuyou ga Arimasu.

I'm trying to get more fresh fruits and vegetables in my diet.
私は食事に新鮮な果物や野菜をもっと取り入れようとしています。
Watashi wa Shokuji ni Shinsen Na kudamono ya yasai o Motto toriireyou to Shite imasu.

I'm feeling more positive and happy since incorporating mindfulness into my daily routine.
日常生活にマインドフルネスを取り入れてから、よりポジティブで幸福感を感じています。
Nichijou seikatsu ni Maindofurunesu o Toriirete kara, yori Pojitive de koufukukan o Kanjite Imasu.

How do you stay healthy and fit?
健康でフィットな状態を維持するためにはどうしますか？
Kenkou de Fitto na Joutai o iji Suru tame ni wa dou Shimasu ka?

Have you been feeling well lately?
最近調子はいかがですか？
Saikin Choushi Wa ikaga Desu ka?

Do you have any health concerns you'd like to discuss?
話したい健康上の懸念事項はありますか？
Hanashitai kenkou jou no Kenen jikou wa Arimasu ka?

Have you been getting enough sleep lately?
最近十分な睡眠をとっていますか？
Saikin juubun Na suimin o Totte imasu ka?

Do you follow any particular diet or exercise regimen?
特定の食事や運動習慣を守っていますか？
Tokutei no Shokuji ya undou Shuukan o Mamotte imasu ka?

How do you manage stress in your life?
人生におけるストレスの管理方法は何ですか？
Jinsei ni okeru Sutoresu no Kanri houhou wa Nanidesu ka?

Do you take any vitamins or supplements to support your health?
健康をサポートするためにビタミンやサプリメントを摂取して
いますか？
Kenkou o sapooto suru Tame ni bitamin ya Sapurimento o Sesshu shite
Imasu ka?

# DESCRIBING JOBS AND PROFESSIONS

I work in the tech industry.
私はテクノロジー業界で働いています。
Watashi wa Tekunorojii Gyoukai de Hataraiteimasu

I'm a lawyer.
私は弁護士です。
Watashi wa Bengoshi Desu

I'm a doctor.
私は医師です。
Watashi Wa ishi Desu

I'm a teacher.
私は教師です。
Watashi wa kyoushi Desu

I'm an accountant.
私は会計士です。
Watashi wa Kaikeishi Desu

I'm an engineer.
私はエンジニアです。
Watashi wa enjinia desu

I work in finance.
私は金融業界で働いています。
Watashi wa kin'you Gyoukai de Hataraiteimasu

I'm a journalist.
私はジャーナリストです。
Watashi wa Jaanarisuto Desu

I'm a musician.
私は音楽家です。
Watashi Wa ongakuka Desu

I'm an artist.
私はアーティストです。
Watashi Wa aatisuto Desu

I'm a chef.
私はシェフです。
Watashi wa Shefu Desu

I work in marketing.
私はマーケティングに従事しています。
Watashi wa Maaketingu ni juuji Shiteimasu

I'm a salesperson.
私は営業職です。
Watashi wa Eigyoushoku Desu

I'm a software developer.
私はソフトウエア開発者です。
Watashi wa Sofutowea Kaihatsusha Desu

I work in customer service.
私はカスタマーサービスに従事しています。
Watashi wa kasutamaa saabisu ni juuji shiteimasu

I'm a graphic designer.
私はグラフィックデザイナーです。
Watashi wa Gurafikku Dezainaa Desu

I'm a writer.
私は作家です。
Watashi wa Sakka Desu

I'm a consultant.
私はコンサルタントです。
Watashi wa Konsarutanto Desu

I work in the tech industry.
私はテクノロジー業界で働いています。
Watashi wa Tekunorojii gyoukai De Hataraiteimasu

I'm a lawyer.
私は弁護士です。
Watashi wa Bengoshi Desu

I'm a doctor.
私は医師です。
Watashi wa Ishi Desu

I'm a teacher.
私は教師です。
Watashi wa Kyoushi Desu

I'm an accountant.
私は会計士です。
Watashi wa Kaikeishi Desu

I'm an engineer.
私はエンジニアです。
Watashi wa Enjinia Desu

I work in finance.
私は金融業界で働いています。
Watashi wa kin'you gyoukai de hataraiteimasu

What do you do for a living?
あなたは何の仕事をしていますか？
Anata wa Nan No shigoto wo Shiteimasu ka?

What kind of work do you do?
あなたはどんな仕事をしていますか？
Anata wa Donna Shigoto wo Shiteimasu ka?

Can you describe your job?
あなたの仕事について説明していただけますか？
Anata No shigoto ni Tsuite setsumei Shite itadakemasu ka?

I work in human resources.
私は人事部で働いています。
Watashi wa jinjibu de Hataraiteimasu.

I'm a project manager.
私はプロジェクトマネージャーです。
Watashi wa Purojekuto Manējā desu.

I'm a social worker.
私はソーシャルワーカーです。
Watashi wa Sōsharu Wākā desu.

I work in public relations.
私は広報部で働いています。
Watashi wa kōhōbu de Hataraiteimasu.

I'm a nurse.
私は看護師です。
Watashi wa kangoshi Desu.

I'm a scientist.
私は科学者です。
Watashi wa Kagakusha Desu.

I'm a researcher.
私は研究者です
Watashi wa kenkyūsha desu.

I'm a therapist.
私はセラピストです。
Watashi wa Serapisuto Desu.

I work in hospitality.
私はホスピタリティ業界で働いています。
Watashi wa Hosupitariti Gyōkai de Hataraiteimasu.

I'm a real estate agent.
私は不動産業者です。
Watashi wa Fudōsan Gyōsha Desu.

I'm a financial advisor.
私はファイナンシャルアドバイザーです。
Watashi wa Fainansharu Adobaizā Desu.

I'm a pharmacist.
私は薬剤師です。
Watashi wa Yakuzaishi Desu.

Can you describe your job?
あなたの仕事について説明していただけますか？
Anata no shigoto ni Tsuite Setsumei shite Itadakemasu ka?

What are your main duties and responsibilities?
あなたの主な業務内容は何ですか？
Anata no Omo na gyōmu naiyō wa Nan Desu ka?

What kind of skills and qualifications are required for your job?
あなたの仕事に必要なスキルや資格は何ですか？
Anata No shigoto ni hitsuyō na Sukiru ya shikaku wa Nan Desu ka?

What do you like about your job?
あなたの仕事の好きな点は何ですか？
Anata no Shigoto no Sukina ten wa Nan Desu ka?

What do you find challenging about your job?
あなたの仕事で難しいと感じる点は何ですか？
Anata no Shigoto de Muzukashii to Kanjiru ten wa nan Desu ka?

How long have you been working in this field?
あなたはこの分野でどのくらい働いていますか？
Anata wa Kono bun'ya De dono kurai Hataraite imasu ka?

What made you choose this profession?

あなたがこの職業を選んだ理由は何ですか？

Anata ga kono Shokugyō wo Eranda riyū wa Nan Desu ka?

# GIVING AND RECEIVING INSTRUCTIONS

Please do this.
これをしてください
Kore wo shite Kudasai

Could you please do this?
これをしていただけますか
Kore wo shite Itadakemasu ka?

Would you mind doing this?
これをやっていただけませんか
Kore wo Yatte Itadakemasen ka?

I'd like you to do this.
これをしていただきたいです
Kore wo Shite itadakitai Desu

Can you do this for me?
これを私のためにできますか
Kore wo watashi No tame ni Dekimasu ka?

It's important that you do this.
これをすることが重要です
Kore wo Suru koto Ga juuyou Desu

Don't forget to do this.
これを忘れないでください
Kore wo Wasurenai de Kudasai

Make sure you do this.
これをするように確認してください
Kore wo suru you Ni kakunin shite Kudasai

You need to do this.
これをする必要があります
Kore wo suru Hitsuyou ga Arimasu

This is what you should do.
これをすべきです
Kore wo Subeki Desu

Sure, I can do that.
もちろん、できます
Mochiron, Dekimasu

Of course, I'll do it right away.
もちろん、すぐにやります
Mochiron, Sugu ni Yarimasu

Absolutely, I'll get right on it.
絶対に、すぐにやります
Zettai ni, Sugu ni Yarimasu

No problem, I can do that.
問題ありません、やれます
Mondai Arimasen, Yaremasu

I understand, I'll do it.
分かりました、やります
Wakarimashita, Yarimasu

Okay, I'll make sure to do that.
わかりました、確実にやります
Wakarimashita, kakujitsu Ni yarimasu

Consider it done.
やります
Yarimasu

I'll take care of it.
任せてください
Makasete Kudasai

Right away, I'll do it.
すぐにやります
Sugu Ni Yarimasu

Yes, I can do that for you.
はい、できます
Hai, Dekimasu

Can you explain that again?
もう一度説明してもらえますか
Mou ichido Setsumei Shite Moraemasu ka?

Could you give me more detail on that?
もっと詳しく説明していただけますか
Motto kuwashiku setsumei Shite itadakemasu ka?

I'm not sure I understand, can you please explain?
分かりません、説明していただけますか
Wakarimasen, Setsumei shite Itadakemasu ka?

Just to clarify, you want me to do this?
確認ですが、これをやってほしいということですか？
Kakunin desu Ga, kore wo Yatte hoshii to iu Koto Desu ka?

Do you mean that I should do this first?
それは最初にやるべきことだということですか？
Sore wa Saisho ni yaru Beki koto da to iu koto Desu ka?

Sorry, I missed that part, can you repeat it?
すみません、その部分を聞き逃してしまいました。もう一度言っていただけますか？
Sumimasen, sono Bubun wo kikinogashite Shimaimashita. Mou ichido itte itadakemasu ka?

Sorry, ik heb dat deel gemist, kun je het herhalen?
すみません、その部分を聞き逃してしまいました。もう一度言っていただけますか？
Sumimasen, sono Bubun Wo kikinogashite Shimaimashita. Mou ichido itte itadakemasu ka?

Sorry, ik HEHDB AHT dehl GHEH-mist, kun yuh het heh-RHAAL-en?
すみません、その部分を聞き逃してしまいました。もう一度言っていただけますか？
Sumimasen, sono Deel Wo kikinogashite Shimaimashita. Mou ichido itte itadakemasu ka?

Can you give me an example of what you mean?
例を教えていただけますか？
Rei wo Oshiete Itadakemasu ka?

Can you explain the reasoning behind that?
その理由を説明していただけますか？
Sono Riyuu wo setsumei Shite Itadakemasu ka?

Just to be clear, you want me to do this now?
確認ですが、今すぐこれをやってほしいということですか？
Kakunin desu ga, ima sugu kore wo yatte hoshii to iu koto desu ka?

Can you show me how to do this?
これのやり方を教えていただけますか？
Kore no Uarikata wo Oshiete Itadakemasu ka?

Please take out the trash.
ゴミを出してください
Gomi wo Dashite Kudasai

Close the door behind you when you leave
出るときにドアを閉めてください
Deru toki ni doa wo shimete kudasai

Turn left at the stop sign
ストップサインで左に曲がってください
Sutoppu Sain de Hidari ni Magatte kudasai

Got it, I'll take out the trash.
分かりました、ゴミを出します
Wakarimashita, Gomi wo Dashimasu

Okay, I'll remember to close the door
わかりました、ドアを閉めるのを覚えておきます
Wakarimashita, Doa wo shimeru No wo oboete Okimasu

Turn left at the stop sign, got it
ストップサインで左に曲がるんですね、分かりました
Sutoppu Sain de hidari ni Magaru n desu ne, Wakarimashita

# EXPRESSING UNCERTAINTY AND PROBABILITY

It's hard to say.
言い難いです。
Ii-gatai Desu.

I'm not sure.
分かりません。
Wakarimasen.

I don't know for Certain.
確証がありません。
Kakushou Ga Arimasen.

It could go either way.
どちらに転ぶかわかりません。
Dochira ni Korobu ka Wakarimasen.

It's anyone's guess.
誰にでも分かりません。
Dare ni Demo Wakarimasen.

It's a toss-up.
五分五分です。
Gobu-Gobu Desu.

How likely is it that...?
どの程度の可能性がありますか？
Dono teido No kanousei ga Arimasu ka?

Do you think there's a chance that...?
の可能性はあると思いますか？
No kanousei Wa aru to Omoimasu ka?

What are the odds of...?
どのような確率ですか？
Dono you na Kakuritsu Desu ka?

Is it possible that...?
可能性があるでしょうか？
Kanousei Ga aru Deshou ka?

Could it be that...?
かもしれませんね。
kamoshiremasen Ne.

Do you have any idea whether...?
かどうか分かりますか？
Ka dou ka Wakarimasu ka?

Would you say it's probable that...?
それは起こりそうだと言えますか？
Sore wa Okorisou da to Iemasu ka?

Is there a good chance that...?
良い可能性がありますか？
Yoi Kanousei ga Arimasu ka?

What's the likelihood of...?
どの程度の確率がありますか？
Dono teido No kakuritsu Ga arimasu ka?

How uncertain are you about...?
どの程度不確かですか？
Dono teido fukakka Desu ka?

There's a chance that...
可能性があります。
Kanousei Ga Arimasu.

There's a possibility that...
可能性があります。
Kanousei Ga Arimasu.

It's not out of the question.
考えられないことではありません。
Kangaerarenai koto De wa Arimasen.

It's a long shot.
かなり不可能です
Kanari Fukanou Desu.

I'm not convinced.
確信が持てません　。
Kakushin Ga Motemasen.

It's too soon to tell.
まだわかりません。
Mada Wakarimasen.

It's up in the air.
不透明です。
Futoumei desu.

It's uncertain.
不確かです。
Fukakka Desu.

I have my doubts.
疑問があります。
Gimon Ga Arimasu.

It's questionable.
疑わしいです。
Utagawashii desu.

It's debatable.
議論の余地がある。
Giron No yochI Ga aru

I'm on the fence about it.
決めかねている。
Kimetakane te Iru

It's a gamble.
博打だ。
Bakuchi Da

It's not a sure thing.
確実なことではない。
Kakujitsn Na koto Dewa Nai

It's not guaranteed.
保証されていない。
Hoshou Sarete Inai

It's possible, but unlikely.
可能性はあるが、あまり期待できない。
Kanousei Wa aru Ga, Amari kitai Dekinai

It's a remote possibility.
ほとんどありえない可能性がある。
Hotondo Arienai Kanousei Ga aru

It's more likely than not.
多分そうだろう。
Tabun sou Darou

It's probable.
ありそうだ。
Arisou Da

There's a good chance that...
大いにありそうだ。
OoIni ari sou Da

It's highly likely.
非常にありそうだ。
HIJou ni Ari sou Da

It's almost certain.
**ほぼ確実だ。**
Hobo Kakujitsu Da

I'm fairly confident.
**かなり自信がある。**
Kanari jishin Ga aru

I'm reasonably certain.
**比較的確信がある。**
Hikakuteki kKakushin Ga aru

# SKILLS

I am experienced in...
経験がある
Keiken Ga aru

I am qualified and capable of...
資格があり、能力がある
Shikaku ga ari, Nōryoku ga aru

I am highly proficient in...
高度に熟練している
Kōdo ni Jukuren Shiteiru

I possess exceptional expertise in...
卓越した専門知識を持っている
Takuei shita senmon Chishiki wo Motteiru

Communication skills
コミュニケーションスキル
Komyunikēshon sukiru

Problem-solving skills
問題解決能力
Mondai Kaiketsu Nōryoku

Teamwork
チームワーク
Chīmuwāku

Time management
タイムマネジメント
Taimumanējimento

Leadership
リーダーシップ
Rīdāshippu

Customer service
顧客サービス
Kokyaku Sābisu

Creativity
創造性
Sōzōsei

Attention to detai
l 細部への注意
Saibu e No Chūi

Sales skills
営業スキル
Eigyō Sukiru

Marketing skills
マーケティングスキル
Māketingu Sukiru

Financial management
財務管理
Zaimu Kanri

# FAMILY

How many siblings do you have?
きょうだいは何人いますか？
Kyoudai wa Nan-Nin Imasu ka?

Are you the oldest, middle, or youngest child?
あなたは一番上、真ん中、一番下の子供ですか？
Anata wa ichiban ue, Man'naka, ichiban Shita no kodomo Desu ka?

What are your parents' occupations?
ご両親はどんなお仕事をされていますか？
Goryoushin wa Donna Oshigoto wo Sarete imasu ka?

Do you have any step-siblings or half-siblings?
継 siblingsや異母 siblingsはいますか？
Tsugiki Siblings ya Ihosiblings wa Imasu ka?

What is your family's cultural background?
あなたの家族の文化的な背景は何ですか？
Anata no kazoku no Bunkateki na Haikei wa nan Desu ka?

Do you have any family traditions?
あなたの家族に伝わる伝統はありますか？
Anata no kazoku Ni tsutawaru Dentou wa arimasu ka?

What is your relationship like with your parents?
両親との関係はどのようなものですか？
Ryoushin to no Kankei wa Dono youna mono Desu ka?

Do you have any nieces or nephews?
あなたには姪や甥がいますか？
Anata ni wa Mei ya oi Ga imasu ka?

Are your grandparents still alive?
おばあちゃん、おじいちゃんはまだ生きていますか？
Obaachan, Ojiichan wa Mada ikite Imasu ka?

Where do your parents or grandparents come from?
ご両親や祖父母はどこから来ましたか？
Goryoushin ya So-fubo wa Doko kara Kimashita ka?

Do you have any family members who live abroad?
外国に住んでいる家族はいますか？
Gaikoku Ni sunde iru Kazoku wa Imasu ka?

What is your family's religion or spiritual beliefs?
あなたの家族の宗教や精神的信念は何ですか？
Anata no kazoku No shuukyou ya Seishinteki Shin'nen wa nan Desu ka?

How often do you see your extended family members?
遠くの家族に会う頻度はどのくらいですか？
Tooku no kazoku ni Au hindo wa Dono kurai Desu ka?

Do you have any family pets?
家族でペットを飼っていますか？
Kazoku de Petto wo katte Imasu ka?

What family member you are closest to?
一番親しい家族は誰ですか？
Ichiban Shitashii Kazoku wa dare Desu ka?

What is your family's favorite dish?
家族のお気に入りの料理は何ですか？
Kazoku no Okiniiri no ryouri wa Nanidesu ka?

Do you have any artists or musicians in the family
家族に芸術家や音楽家がいますか？
Kazoku ni Geijutsuka ya Ongakuka ga Imasu ka?

Do you have any family heirlooms or sentimental objects?
家族の形見や思い出の品はありますか？
Kazoku no Katami ya omoide No shina wa Arimasu ka?

What is the most important lesson you learned from your family?
家族から学んだ最も重要な教訓は何ですか？
Kazoku kara Mananda mottomo juuyou Na kyoukun wa Nanidesu ka?

Has anyone in your family served in the military?
家族に軍務に就いた人がいますか？
Kazoku ni Gunmu ni Tsuita hito ga Imasu ka?

What is the biggest challenge faced by your family?
家族が直面した最大の課題は何ですか？
Kazoku Ga chokumen Shita saidai No kadai wa Nanidesu ka?

Do you have any entrepreneurs or business owners in the family?
家族に起業家やビジネスオーナーがいますか？
Kazoku ni kigyouka Ya Bijinesu Oonaa ga Imasu ka?

What is your family's stance on important social issues
家族の重要な社会問題に対する立場は何ですか？
Kazoku no juuyou Na Shakai mondai ni Taisuru tachiba wa Nanidesu ka?

Do you have any family members who are educators or involved in academia?
家族に教育者や学者がいますか？
Kazoku ni kyouikusha ya Gakusha ga Imasu ka?

What is your family's religious or spiritual background?
家族の宗教的または精神的な背景は何ですか？
Kazoku no shuukyouteki Matawa seishinteki Na haikei wa Nanidesu ka?

Are there any family members who are involved in charitable or volunteer work?
家族にボランティア活動や慈善活動に関わっている人がいますか？
Kazoku ni Borantia katsudou Ya jizen Katsudou ni kakawatte iru hito Ga imasu ka?

What is the most memorable family vacation or trip you have taken together?

家族で一緒に行った最も思い出深い旅行は何ですか？

Kazoku de issho Ni itta mottomo Omoide fukai ryokou wa Nanidesu ka?


Do you have any family members who have achieved something noteworthy or remarkable?

家族に注目すべき成し遂げた人がいますか？

Lazoku ni Chuumoku subeki Nasshi tageta hito Ga imasu ka?


What is your family's opinion on marriage and relationships?

家族の結婚や人間関係に対する考え方は何ですか？

kazoku no kekkon ya ningen kankei ni taisuru kangaekata wa Nanidesu ka?


Do you have any family traditions or customs that are unique to your family?

家族だけの独自の伝統や習慣はありますか？

Kazoku dake No Dokujino Dentou ya Shuukan Wa Arimasu ka?


Who in your family is the best storyteller?

家族で一番上手な話し手は誰ですか？

Kazoku De ichiban Umai hanashite wa Dare desu ka?


Do you have any family members who are skilled in a particular craft or hobby?

家族に特定の工芸品や趣味に長けた人がいますか？

Kazoku ni Tokutei no Kougeihin ya Shumi ni taketa Hito ga imasu ka?


What is the most interesting fact about your family history?

家族の歴史で最も興味深い事実は何ですか？

Kazoku no rekishi De mottomo kyoumibukai Jijitsu wa Nanidesu ka?


Are there any family recipes or dishes that have been passed down through generations?

家族の代々伝わるレシピや料理はありますか？

Kazoku no dai-Dai tsutawaru Reshipi ya ryouri wa Arimasu ka?

What is your family's stance on education and lifelong learning?

家族の教育や終生学習に対するスタンスは何ですか？

Kazoku no kyouiku ya Shuushou Gakushuu ni taisuru Sutansu wa Nanidesu ka?

# BUSINESS NEGOTIATION

Let's start with the initial proposal.
最初の提案から始めましょう。
Saisho No teian kara Hajimemashou

We need to identify our common interests.
共通の利益を特定する必要があります。
Kyoutsuu No rieki wo tokutei Suru hitsuyou ga Arimasu

Can we find a middle ground that works for both parties?
両者にとってうまくいく折衷案を見つけることができますか？
Ryousha ni totte umaku iku Chouchuu-an wo Mitsukeru koto ga
Dekimasu ka?

Let's discuss the timeline for implementation.
実施のタイムラインについて話し合いましょう。
jisshi No taimurain ni Tsuite hanashi Aimashou

We need to consider the budget constraints.
予算の制約を考慮する必要があります。
Yosan No seiyaku wo kouryo Suru hitsuyou ga Arimasu

Can we negotiate on the payment terms?
支払い条件について交渉できますか？
Shiharai jouken ni Tsuite koushou Dekimasu ka?

Let's discuss the scope of the project.
プロジェクトの範囲について話し合いましょう。
Purojekuto No han'i ni tsuite hanashi Aimashou

We need to clarify the roles and responsibilities of each party.
各当事者の役割と責任を明確にする必要があります。
Kaku toujisha no yakuwari to Sekinin wo Meikaku ni suru Hitsuyou ga
Arimasu

Can we discuss the potential risks and challenges?
潜在的なリスクや課題について話し合えますか？
Senzaiteki na risuku ya kadai ni tsuite hanashiaemasu ka?

Let's explore options for mutual benefit.
相互利益のための選択肢を探りましょう。
Sougo Rieki no Tame no sentakushi wo Sagurimashou

Let's brainstorm ideas and solutions.
アイデアや解決策をブレインストーミングしましょう。
Aidea ya Kaiketsusaku wo Bureinsuto-Mingu Shimashou

We need to come up with a feasible plan.
実現可能な計画を立てる必要があります。
Jitsugen kanou na Kei-Ka-ku wo tateru Hitsuyou Ga Arimasu

Can we consider alternative options?
代替案を考慮できますか？
Dai-tai-an wo kou-ryo Ekimasu ka?

Let's analyze the market trends and competition.
市場のトレンドや競合を分析しましょう。
Shijou No Torendo ya Kyou-Gou wo Bunseki Shimashou

We need to reach a compromise that satisfies both parties.
両者に満足できる妥協点を見つける必要があります。
Ryousha ni Manzoku Dekiru Dakyou-ten wo Mitsukeru Hitsuyou ga Arimasu

Can we negotiate the terms of the contract?
契約条件を交渉できますか？
Keiyaku Jouken wo Koushou Dekimasu ka?

Let's review the key points of the agreement.
契約書の要点を確認しましょう。
Keiyaku-Sho No You-ten wo Kakunin Shimashou

We need to make sure that the deal is mutually beneficial.
双方にとってメリットのある取引であることを確認する必要が
あります。
Souhou ni totte Meritto no aru TorI-Hiki de aru koto wo kakunin Suru
hitsuyou ga Arimasu

Can we discuss the terms of payment in detail?
支払い条件について詳細に話し合えますか？
Shiharai Jouken ni tsuite Shousai ni Hanashiaemasu ka?

We need to find a solution that meets everyone's needs.
全員のニーズに合った解決策を見つける必要があります。
Zenin no NI-Zu ni atta Kaiketsusaku wo Mitsukeru hitsuyou ga Arimasu

Can we discuss the pricing and costs involved?
価格やコストについて話し合えますか？
Kakaku ya Kosuto Ni tsuite Hanashiaemasu ka?

We need to review and finalize the contract.
契約書をレビューし、最終的に決定する必要があります。
Keiyakusho Wo rebii Shi, Saishuuteki ni Kettei suru Hitsuyou Ga
arimasu

Can we agree on the terms and conditions?
条件に同意できますか？
jouken ni doui Dekimasu ka?

We need to negotiate a win-win situation.
ウィンウィンの状況を交渉する必要があります。
Win-win no Joukyou wo koushou suru itsuyou Ga Arimasu

Can we discuss the deliverables and deadlines?
納品物と納期について話し合えますか？
Nouhinbutsu to Nouki ni tsuite Hanashiaemasu ka?

# DESCRIBING ARTWORK

The painting is very vivid and colorful.
絵画はとても生き生きとして色彩が豊かです。
Kaiga wa Totemo ikikito Shite shikisai Ga yutakadesu

The sculpture has intricate details and textures.
彫刻には細かいディテールとテクスチャがあります。
Choukoku ni wa komakai diteeru To tekusucha ga Arimasu

The artwork is very abstract and open to interpretation.
作品は非常に抽象的で解釈の余地があります。
Sakuhin wa hijou ni Chuushouteki De kaishaku no yochi ga Arimasu

The artist used a lot of contrast to create a dramatic effect.
アーティストは対比を多用して劇的な効果を作り出しました。
Aatisuto wa taihi wo tayou shite Gekiteki na kouka wo
Tsukuridashimashita

The piece has a lot of movement and energy.
作品には多くの動きとエネルギーがあります。
Sakuhin ni wa Ooku no ugoki to Enerugii ga Arimasu

The colors in the painting are very bold and striking.
絵画の色はとても大胆で印象的です。
kaiga No iro wa totemo Daitan de inshouteki Desu

The lines in the drawing are very fluid and dynamic.
絵の描画の線は非常に流れるようでダイナミックです。
E no byouga No sen wa hijou ni Nagareru you de Dainamikku Desu

The artwork has a very serene and peaceful quality to it.
作品には非常に静かで平和的な質があります。
Sakuhin ni wa Hijou ni shizuka de Heiwateki na shitsu ga Arimasu

The composition of the piece is very balanced and harmonious.
作品の構成は非常にバランスが取れて調和的です。
Sakuhin no Kousei wa Hijou ni baransu Ga torete chouwateki Desu

The texture in the artwork is very rough and tactile.
作品のテクスチャは非常に荒々しく触感があります。
Sakuhin No tekusucha wa hijou Ni araarashiku Shokkan ga Arimasu

The use of light and shadow in the painting is very impressive.
絵画における明暗の使い方は非常に印象的です。
kaiga ni okeru Meian no Tsukaikata wa hijou Ni inshouteki Desu

The piece has a very dark and ominous tone to it.
作品には非常に暗く不吉なトーンがあります。
Sakuhin ni wa hijou Ni kuraku fukitsu Na toon ga Arimasu

The subject matter of the artwork is very thought-provoking.
作品の主題は非常に考えさせられるものです。
Sakuhin No shudai wa hijou ni kangae Saserareru Mono Desu

The painting is very realistic and lifelike.
この 絵 は 非常 に リアル で 生き 生き と しています。
Kono E wa hijou Ni riaru de iki-iki to Shiteimasu.

The artist used a lot of texture to create depth in the artwork.
芸術 家 は 肌 触 り を たくさん 使 用 して 作品 に 奥行き
を 生み出しました。
Geijutsuka wa hadazawari wo Takusan shiyou Shite sakuhin ni Okuyuki
wo Umidashimashita.

The piece is very abstract and experimental in its approach.
この 作品 は 非常 に 抽象 的 で 実験 的 な アプローチ を 取
って います。
Kono sakuhin wa Hijou ni chuushou-teki de jikken-teki Na apurouchi
wo totte Imasu.

The sculpture has a very smooth and polished finish.
彫刻 は 非常 に 滑 ら か で 磨 か れ た 仕上げ と なっ て い ます。
Choukoku wa hijou ni Nameraka de Migakareta shiage to Natteimasu.

The colors in the piece complement each other very well.
作品 の 色 は 互い に 非常 に 調和 し て い ます。
Sakuhin No iro wa Tagai ni hijou Ni chouwa Shiteimasu.

The painting has a very dreamlike quality to it.
この 絵 に は 非常 に 夢 のよう な 特質 が ある。
Kono E ni wa hijou ni yume No you na tokushitsu Ga aru.

The lines in the artwork are very sharp and precise.
作品 の 線 は 非常 に 鋭利 で 正確 です。
Sakuhin no Sen wa hijou Ni eiri de seikaku Desu.

The artist used a lot of symbolism in the piece.
芸術 家 は 作品 に 大量 の 象徴 主義 を 使 用 し まし た。
Geijutsuka wa sakuhin ni Tairyou no shouchuu shugi wo Shiyou shimashita.

The piece has a very futuristic and otherworldly feel to it.
この 作品 は 非常 に 未来 的 で 異世界 的 な 雰囲気 を 持 っ て い ます。
Kono sakuhin wa hijou ni mirai-teki de i-sekai-teki na Fun'iki wo Motteimasu.

The use of color in the artwork is very bold and daring.
作品 の 色 の 使い方 は 非常 に 大胆 で 思い切っ た もの です。
Sakuhin No iro no Tsukaikata wa hijou Ni daitan de Omoikitatta mono Desu.

The piece has a very playful and whimsical tone to it.
この 作品 は 非常 に 楽しげ で 気まぐれ な 雰囲気 が 漂っ て い ます。
Kono sakuhin wa Hijou ni tanoshige de kimagure na Fun'iki ga Tadayotteimasu.

The sculpture has a very dynamic and energetic feel to it.
彫刻 は 非常 に ダイナミック で エネルギッシュ な 雰囲気 を 持っ て い ます。
Choukoku wa hijou ni Dainamikku de Enerugisshu na fun'iki wo Motteimasu.

The use of light in the artwork creates a very dramatic effect.
作品の中の光の使い方は、非常にドラマティックな効果を生み出しています。
Sakuhin no naka No hikari no Tsukai-kata wa, Hijō ni Doramatikku na kōka o Umidasu shite imasu.

The piece has a very raw and emotional quality to it.
作品には、非常に生々しく感情的な質があります。
Sakuhin Ni wa, hijō ni Namamugi Shiku kanjō-teki na Shitsu ga arimasu.

The artist used a lot of contrast to create a striking visual impact.
アーティストは、コントラストを多用して、印象的な視覚的なインパクトを作り出しました。
Aatistto wa, kontorasuto o tayō shite, inshō-teki na shikakuteki na inpakuto o tsukuridashimashita.

The piece has a very nostalgic and sentimental feeling to it.
作品には、非常にノスタルジックでセンチメンタルな雰囲気があります。
Sakuhin ni wa, hijō Ni nosutarujikku de Senchimentaru Na fun'iki ga Arimasu.

The artwork has a very whimsical and playful quality to it.
作品には、非常に気まぐれで遊び心のある質があります。
Sakuhin Ni wa, hijō ni kimagure de Asobigokoro No aru shitsu ga Arimasu.

The colors used in the painting are very vibrant and eye-catching.
絵画に使用されている色は、非常に鮮やかで目を引くものです。
Kaiga ni shiyō Sarete iru iro wa, hijō ni Azayaka de me O hiku mono Desu.

The artwork has a very ethereal and dreamlike quality to it.
作品には、非常に幻想的で夢のような質があります。
Sakuhin ni wa, hijō ni Gensō-teki de yume no yō Na shitsu ga Arimasu.

The use of texture in the sculpture adds an interesting tactile element.
彫刻における質感の使用は、興味深い触覚的要素を加えています。
Chōkoku ni Okeru shitsukan No Shiyō wa, Kyōmibukai Shokkakuteki yōso O kuwaete imasu.

The piece has a very Contemporary and Modern feel to it.
作品には、非常に現代的でモダンな感じがあります。
Sakuhin Ni wa, hijō ni Gendai-teki De modan Na kanji ga Arimasu.

# WATCHING SOCCER

Great pass! That was brilliant!
素晴らしいパスだ！すばらしかった！
Subarashii Pasu da! Su-ba-Ra-shi-ka-Tta!

Come on, ref! That was a violation!
ちょっと、レフェリー！ファールだったよ！
Chotto, referee! Fa-ru datta yo!

What a goal! Absolutely incredible!
すごいゴールだ！まったく信じられない！
Sugoi Go-ru da! Mat-ta-ku shin-ji-ra-re-Nai!

Offside! He was clearly offside.
オフサイド！明らかにオフサイドだった。
Ofusaido! A-kira-ka-ni Ofusaido Datta!

Great save from the keeper!
ゴールキーパーの素晴らしいセーブだ！
Go-ruki-Pa- no su-Ba-ra-shii se-Bu da!

Stand up, that was hardly an offense!
立ち上がって、それはほとんど反則じゃない！
Ta-chi-a-Gat-te, Sore wa ho-to-do Han-soku ja-nai!

What are you doing? You had an open shot!
何してるんだよ？シュートのチャンスがあったのに！
Nani shi-te-ru n da yo? Shu-to No chan-su Ga at-ta Noni!

That was a bad decision by the linesman.
ラインズマンの判断が悪かった。
Rai-nzu-Man no han-da-n ga Waru-kat-ta.

The defense needs to tighten up, they give away too much space.
守備陣はもっと固くならなければならない、スペースをあまりにも与えすぎる。
Shubi-jin wa Mot-to kata-kunara-na-kere-ba-na-ra-nai, su-Pesu wo a-ma-ri-Ni-mo a-tae-su-giru.

That was hardly a yellow card, the ref is too strict.
イエローカードはほとんどなかった、レフェリーは厳しすぎる。
Ie-ro- ka-Do wa ho-to-Do na-ka-tta, Referee wa ki-Bo-shi-su-giru.

What a miss! How could he not score that?
なんてことだ！あのシュートが決まらなかったのか！
Nan-te ko-to da! Ano shu-to Ga ke-ma-ra-na-kat-ta No ka!

That was a perfect slide, well done!
完璧なスライディングだった、よくやった！
Kan-pe-ki Na su-rai-di-n-Gu da-Tta, yo-ku ya-tta!

He's not on a roll today, he needs to raise the level.
彼は今日調子が上がっていない、レベルを上げる必要がある。
Ka-re wa kyo-Cho-shi ga a-Gat-te-i-na-i, re-Beru wo a-ge-ru Hitsu-yo Ga aru.

Fantastic control through the midfield, they dominate possession.
ミッドフィールドを通しての素晴らしいコントロール、彼らはポゼッションを支配している。
Midofirudo wo to-shi-te no Su-ba-ra-shii kon-To-ro-ru, ka-ra-ra wa Po-ze-shon wo Shi-hai-shi-te-i-Ru.

That was a weak attempt, he needs to put more power behind the ball.
それは弱い試みだった、彼はもっとパワーを込める必要がある。
Sore wa yowa-i ko-ko-ro-Mi da-tta, ka-re wa Mot-to pa-wa- wo ko-Me-ru Hitsu-yo Ga aru.

That was a clear penalty kick, good decision by the referee.
それは明らかな だった、レフェリーの判断は正しかった。
Sore wa A-kira-ka-na PK datta, Referee no Han-Da-n wa ta-Da-Shi-kat-ta.

190

The goalkeeper played a great game today, he keeps the team going.
　ゴールキーパーは今日素晴らしいプレーをした、彼がチームを
支えてい
Go-ruki-pa- wa Kyo-su-ba-ra-Shii pu-re- Wo Shi-ta, ka-re Ga Chi-mu wo
sa-e-Te-i-ru.

The players need to be smarter, they give away too many unnecessary
free kicks.
　選手たちはもっと賢くなる必要がある、無駄なフリーキックを
あまりにも与えすぎる。
Senshu-ta-Chi wa mot-to ka-Shi-ku-na-ru Hitsu-yo ga aru, mu-Da-na
fu-ri-ki-ku wo a-Ma-ri-ni-mo a-Tae-su-Giru.

The keeper didn't stand a chance.
ゴールキーパーには勝機がなかった。
Go-ruki-pa- ni wa Shou-ki Ga na-kat-ta.

# VISITING A BARBER OR HAIRSTYLIST

Can you give me a trim?
散髪してもらえますか？
Sanpatsu Shite Moraemasu ka?

I want to go shorter, can you help me with that?
もう少し短くして欲しいのですが、手伝っていただけますか？
Mou sukoshi Mijikaku shite Hoshii no desu ga, Tetsudatte itadakemasu ka?

Can you give me a buzz cut?
バリカンで坊主にしてもらえますか？
Barikan de Bouzu ni shite Moraemasu ka?

Can you give me a fade?
フェードカットにしてもらえますか？
Feedo katto ni Shite Moraemasu ka?

I want to keep the length but just tidy it up a bit.
長さはそのままで、少し整えて欲しいのですが。
Nagasa wa sono Mama de, sukoshi Totonoete Hoshii no Desu ga.

Can you add some layers to my hair?
髪にレイヤーを入れてもらえますか？
Kami ni Reiyaa o irete Moraemasu ka?

I want to go for a new style, can you recommend something?
新しいスタイルに挑戦したいのですが、何かおすすめがありますか？
Atarashii sutairu ni Chousen shitai No desu ga, Nanika osusume Ga arimasu ka?

Can you thin out my hair a bit?
髪を少し薄くしてもらえますか？
Kami o Sukoshi usuku Shite moraemasu ka?

Can you give me a side part?
サイドパートにしてもらえますか？
Saido Paato ni shite Moraemasu ka?

Can you give me a messy look?
メッシュな髪型にしてもらえますか？
Messhu na Kamigata ni Shite Moraemasu ka?

I want to keep my curls but just tidy them up a bit.
カールは残したまま、少し整えて欲しいのですが。
Kaaru wa Nokoshita mama, Sukoshi totonoete Hoshii no Desu ga.

Can you help me grow out my hair?
髪を伸ばす手助けをしてもらえますか？
Kami o Nobasu Tedasuke o Shite moraemasu ka?

I want to add some highlights, can you do that?
ハイライトを入れたいのですが、やってもらえますか？
Hairaito O iretai no Desu ga, yatte Moraemasu ka?

Can you give me a sleek, straight look?
スリークでストレートな髪型にしてもらえますか？
Suriku De sutureeto Na kamigata ni shite Moraemasu ka?

I want to go for a bold color, can you help me with that?
大胆な色にしたいのですが、手伝ってもらえますか？
Daitan na iro Ni shitai no Desu ga, Tetsudatte Moraemasu ka?

Can you give me a perm?
パーマをかけてもらえますか？
Paama o Kakete Moraemasu ka?

Can you help me get rid of split ends?
切れ毛を取ってもらえますか？
Kirege o Totte Moraemasu ka?

Can you give me a trim but leave my bangs longer?
トリミングして前髪は長めにしてもらえますか？
Toringu shite Maegami wa Nagame ni Shite Moraemasu ka?

I want to go for a shorter cut but still keep some length, can you help me with that?
長さは残しつつ、ショートヘアにしてもらえますか？
Nagasa wa Nokoshitsutsu, Shooto hea ni shite Moraemasu ka?

Can you help me style my hair for a special occasion?
特別なイベントのために髪型をアレンジしてもらえますか？
Tokubetsu na ibento no tame Ni kamigata o Arenji shite oraemasu ka?

Can you recommend some products to help me style my hair at home?
自宅でのヘアスタイリングに使える商品を教えてもらえますか？
Jitaku de no Hea sutairingu ni Tsukaeru shouhin O oshiete Moraemasu ka?

Can you give me a clean, polished look?
クリーンでポリッシュされた髪型にしてもらえますか？
Kuriin de Porisshu sareta kamigata ni Shite moraemasu ka?

I want to keep my hair long but just add some shape to it.
長さはそのままで、形を整えてもらえますか？
Nagasa wa Sono mama De, katachi O totonoete Moraemasu ka?

Can you give me a textured look?
テクスチャーのある髪型にしてもらえますか？
Tekusuchaa No aru kamigata Ni shite Moraemasu ka?

I want to go for a natural, beachy look.
ナチュラルでビーチ風の印象にしたいです。
Nachuraru de Bii-chi fuu No inshou Ni shitai Desu.

Can you give me a retro, vintage style?
レトロでヴィンテージなスタイルを提案してもらえますか？
Retoro de Vin-te-ji na Sutairu wo Teian shite Morae masu ka?

I want to go for a sleek, professional look.
スマートでプロフェッショナルな印象にしたいです。
Sumaato de Purofesshonaru Na inshou ni Shitai desu.

Can you give me a shaved undercut?
シェイブド・アンダーカットにしてもらえますか？
Sheibudo Andaakatto ni shite Morae masu ka?

Can you help me add volume to my hair?
髪にボリュームを出す方法を教えてください。
Kami ni Boryuumu wo Dasu Houhou wo Oshiete kudasai.

I want to go for a trendy, edgy style.
トレンディでエッジの効いたスタイルにしたいです。
Torendi de Ejji no kiita sutairu Ni shitai Desu.

## SHOPPING AT A GROCERY STORE

Where can I find the milk?
牛乳はどこですか？
Gyuu-Nyuu wa Doko Desu ka?


Do you carry almond milk?
アーモンドミルクは扱っていますか？
Aamonndo miruku wa Atsukatte Imasu ka?


Can you direct me to the bread aisle?
パンの棚はどこですか？
Pan no Tana wa doko Desu ka?


Where can I find fresh produce?
新鮮な農産物はどこにありますか？
Shinsen na Nousanbutsu wa Doko ni Arimasu ka?


Do you have any ripe bananas?
熟れたバナナはありますか？
Ureta Banana wa Arimasu ka?


Where can I find the eggs?
卵はどこにありますか？
Tamago wa Doko ni Arimasu ka?


Do you carry organic produce?
オーガニック農産物は扱っていますか？
Ooganikku Nousanbutsu wa Atsukatte imasu ka?


Can you direct me to the meat department?
肉の売り場はどこですか？
Niku no Uriba wa Doko desu ka?

Where can I find ground beef?
挽肉はどこにありますか？
Hikiniku wa Doko ni Arimasu ka?

Do you have any chicken breasts?
鶏胸肉はありますか？
Tori Muneniku wa Arimasu ka?

Can you tell me where the canned goods are located?
缶詰はどこにありますか？
Kandume wa Doko ni Arimasu ka?

Where can I find the pasta?
パスタはどこにありますか？
Pasuta wa doko ni arimasu ka?

Do you carry gluten-free products?
グルテンフリー商品は扱っていますか？
Guruten furii shouhin wa Atsukatte imasu ka?

Can you direct me to the bakery?
ベーカリーはどこですか？
Beekarii wa Doko Desu ka?

Where can I find fresh baked bread?
焼きたてのパンはどこにありますか？
yakitatenopan wa Doko ni Arimasu ka?

Do you have any bagels left?
ベーグルはまだありますか？
Beeguru wa Mada Arimasu ka?

Can you tell me where the frozen foods are located?
冷凍食品はどこにありますか？
Reitou shokuhin wa Doko ni Arimasu ka?

Where can I find ice cream?
アイスクリームはどこにありますか？
Aisukuriimu wa Doko ni Arimasu ka?

Do you carry any vegan products?
ヴィーガン商品は扱っていますか？
Viigan Shouhin wa Atsukatte imasu ka?

Can you direct me to the deli counter?
デリカウンターはどこですか？
Derikauntaa wa Doko Desu ka?

Where can I find sliced turkey?
スライスターキーはどこにありますか？
Suraisu Taakii wa Doko ni Arimasu ka?

Do you have any freshly made sandwiches?
手作りのサンドイッチはありますか？
Tezukuri No sandoicchi wa Arimasu ka?

Can you tell me where the chips and snacks are located?
ポテトチップスやスナック菓子はどこにありますか？
Poteto Chippusu ya Sunakku kashi wa Doko ni Arimasu ka?

Where can I find potato chips?
ポテトチップスはどこにありますか？
Poteto Chippusu wa Doko ni Arimasu ka?

Do you carry any specialty items such as international foods or spices?
国際料理やスパイスなどの特別な商品は扱っていますか？
Kokusai ryouri ya Supaisu nado no Tokubetsu na Shouhin wa Atsukatte imasu ka?

Where can I find the rice?
米はどこにありますか？
kome wa Doko ni Arimasu ka?

Do you have any quinoa?
キヌアはありますか？
Kinua wa Arimasu ka?

Can you direct me to the seafood department?
魚介類の売り場はどこですか？
Gyokairui No uriba wa Doko desu ka?

Where can I find fresh salmon?
新鮮なサーモンはどこにありますか？
Shinsen na Saamon wa Doko ni Arimasu ka?

Do you carry any sushi-grade fish?
寿司ネタに適した魚は扱っていますか？
Sushi neta ni teki Shita sakana wa Atsukatte imasu ka?

Can you tell me where the cheese is located?
チーズはどこにありますか？
Chiizu wa Doko ni Arimasu ka?

Where can I find cheddar cheese?
チェダーチーズはどこにありますか？
Chedaachiizu wa Doko ni Arimasu ka?

Do you have any goat cheese?
山羊チーズはありますか？
yagi Chiizu wa Arimasu ka?

Can you direct me to the bulk foods section?
まとめ買い商品の売り場はどこですか？
Matomegai shouhin No Uriba wa doko Desu ka?

Where can I find nuts and seeds?
ナッツや種実類はどこにありますか？
Nattsu ya shushitsurui wa Doko ni Arimasu ka?

Do you carry any dried fruits?
ドライフルーツは扱っていますか？
Dorai furuutsu wa Atsukatte Imasu ka?

Can you tell me where the condiments are located?
調味料はどこにありますか？
Choumiryou wa Doko ni Arimasu ka?

Where can I find ketchup?
ケチャップはどこにありますか？
Kechappu wa Doko ni Arimasu ka?

Do you have any mustard?
マスタードはありますか？
Masutaado wa Arimasu ka?

Can you direct me to the beer and wine section?
ビールとワインのコーナーはどこですか？
Bīru to wain No kōnā wa Doko desu ka?

Where can I find red wine?
赤ワインはどこにありますか？
Aka wain wa Doko ni Arimasu ka?

Do you have any craft beer?
クラフトビールはありますか？
Kurafuto Bīru wa Arimasu ka?

Can you tell me where the paper products are located?
紙製品はどこにありますか？
Kamiseihin wa Doko ni Arimasu ka?

Where can I find toilet paper?
トイレットペーパーはどこにありますか？
Toiretto Pēpā wa Doko ni Arimasu ka?

Do you have any paper towels?
ペーパータオルはありますか？
Pēpā Taoru wa Arimasu ka?

Can you direct me to the cleaning supplies section?
掃除用品のコーナーはどこですか？
Sōji yōhin No kōnā wa doko Desu ka?

Where can I find dish soap?
食器用洗剤はどこにありますか？
Shokkiyō senzai wa Doko ni Arimasu ka?

Do you have any laundry detergent?
洗濯洗剤はありますか？
Sentaku Senzai wa Arimasu ka?

Can you tell me where the pet food is located?
ペットフードはどこにありますか？
Petto fūdo wa Doko ni Arimasu ka?

Where can I find cat food?
キャットフードはどこにありますか？
Kyatto Fūdo wa Doko ni Arimasu ka?

# BUYING HOME SUPPLIES

Can you direct me to the baby products section?
ベビー用品コーナーはどこですか？
Bebī yōhin kōnā wa Doko Desu ka?

Where can I find diapers?
おむつはどこにありますか？
Omutsu wa Doko ni Arimasu ka?

Do you carry any organic baby food?
オーガニックのベビーフードはありますか？
Ōganikku No bebi fūdo wa Arimasu ka?

Can you tell me where the pharmacy is located?
薬局はどこにありますか？
Yakkyoku wa Doko ni Arimasu ka?

Where can I find pain relievers?
鎮痛剤はどこにありますか？
Chintsūzai wa Doko ni Arimasu ka?

Do you carry any cough medicine?
咳止めの薬はありますか？
Sekitome No kusuri wa Arimasu ka?

Can you direct me to the cosmetics aisle?
化粧品の売り場はどこですか？
Keshōhin no Uriba wa Doko Desu ka?

Where can I find shampoo?
シャンプーはどこにありますか？
Shanpū wa Doko ni Arimasu ka?

Do you carry any natural or organic beauty products?
ナチュラル・オーガニックの美容製品はありますか？
Nachuraru Oganikku no biyō Seihin wa Arimasu ka?

Can you tell me where the kitchenware is located?
調理器具はどこにありますか？
Chōri kigu wa Doko ni Arimasu ka?

Where can I find pots and pans?
鍋やフライパンはどこにありますか？
Nabe ya furai pan wa Doko ni Arimasu ka?

Do you carry any baking supplies?
ベーキング用品はありますか？
Bēkingu yōhin wa Arimasu ka?

Can you direct me to the electronics section?
家電売り場はどこですか？
Kaden uriba Wa doko Desu ka?

Where can I find headphones?
ヘッドフォンはどこにありますか？
Heddofon wa doko ni arimasu ka?

Do you carry any phone chargers?
スマホ充電器はありますか？
Sumaho jūdenki wa Arimasu ka?

Can you tell me where the office supplies are located?
事務用品はどこにありますか？
Jimu yōhin wa Doko ni Arimasu ka?

Where can I find pens and paper?
ペンや紙はどこにありますか？
Pen ya kami wa Doko ni Arimasu ka?

Made in the USA
Monee, IL
02 June 2024

59289492R00111